REWIRE
Creating a High-Performance Mindset for Personal and Professional Excellence

Copyright © 2025 by Mandy Napier, BSc — www.mindsetforsuccess.com.au

All rights reserved. No part of this book may be produced or utilised in any form or by any means, electronic or mechanical, including photocopying, recording, or by any information storage and retrieval system, without permission in writing from the Publisher.

Published 2025

Publisher: Mandy Napier, BSc, Mindset for Success

Graphic Design & Layout: Mélissa Caron — go-Enki.com

Editor: Richard Burian, MA, MLitt, CELTA — www.richard-burian.com

ISBN: 978-0-9942316-4-2

Self-Help, Mindset, Psychology

Creating a
High-Performance Mindset
for Personal and Professional
Excellence

By Mandy Napier, BSc

Table of Contents

TESTIMONIALS 9

FOREWORD 17

INTRODUCTION 19
The Power of Perspective 20
The Modern Struggle 22
The Path to a High-Performance Mindset 24

CHAPTER 1: WHAT IS A HIGH-PERFORMANCE MINDSET? 29
Defining a High-Performance Mindset 29
The Power of Controlling the Controllables — Craig Tiley's Story ... 30
The Key Traits of a High-Performance Mindset 32
Final Thoughts 35
Key Insights 36

CHAPTER 2: WHY A HIGH-PERFORMANCE MINDSET IS CRITICAL TODAY 39
The Demands of Modern Life 39
Why Change Is Urgent 40
Why a High-Performance Mindset Is the Answer 41
From Deflated to Energised 41
The High-Performance Mindset VALUE Model 42
Understanding the VALUE Model 43
The Six Levels of the VALUE Model 44
Where Do You Sit? 51
Key Insights 52

CHAPTER 3: BARRIERS TO A HIGH-PERFORMANCE MINDSET ... 53
Why Do We Hold Ourselves Back? 53
The Rules of the Mind 55

Common Barriers to a High-Performance Mindset 60
Final Thoughts 66
Key Insights 67

CHAPTER 4: PERSONAL STORIES OF TRANSFORMATION 69

The Seeds of Curiosity and Resilience 70
From the Hunza Valley to the Hawaiian Ironman 72
Client Stories of Transformation 73
Final Thoughts 74
Key Insights 74

CHAPTER 5: THE REWIRE MODEL FOR HIGH-PERFORMANCE 77

Why REWIRE? 77
What Does It Mean to Rewire Your Brain? 78
Harnessing Energy 79
The REWIRE Model Explained 80
The Key Components of the REWIRE Model 86
Key Insights 94
Action Steps 94

CHAPTER 6: BUILDING CLARITY — INSIDE OUT WORK 97

Choosing a Destination 97
Goals 99
CLEARer Goals 100
Creating a Plan 105
The Power of Thoughts 107
Thoughts Become Ingrained Habits 108
My Hawaii Story 109
The Science of Thought and Energy 111
The Positive Self-Talk Optimiser 112
Know What Is Important — Values 114
Discovering Your Core Values 115
Aspirational Values 117
Strengths and Talents 118
Discovering Your Strengths 118

Clarity to Consistency to Impact 121
Final Thoughts 121
Key Insights 122
Action Steps 122

CHAPTER 7: DEVELOPING CONSISTENCY **125**
Habits: The Foundation of Success 126
The Power of Habits 127
The Science of Habits 128
The Role of Dopamine and Rewards 130
Using the Environment To Your Advantage 131
Seven Keys to Successful Habits 134
Mental Habits 135
Emotional Habits 144
Physical Habits 151
Final Thoughts 155
Key Insights 156
Action Steps 156

CHAPTER 8: CREATING IMPACT **157**
Core Energy 158
Thriving in a fast-moving world 159
The Power of Deliberate, Purposeful Practice 162
Small Improvements, Big Results 165
The Essential Role of Feedback 166
The Power of Expectation 168
The Power of Intention 170
The Power of Attention 172
Expanding Thinking 174
The Power of Deep Listening 175
How to Train Your Mind for 10x Thinking 176
Prioritisation 177
Managing Emotions 179
Understanding Stress 180
Befriending Fear 181

Practical Strategies to Manage Stress 183
Mindfulness and Meditation 184
Yawning: A Simple Yet Powerful Brain Reset 186
Harnessing Strengths for Greater Impact 187
Leveraging What You Do Best 190
The Power of Self-Care 192
The Healing Power of Nature 194
The Power of Play 195
Self-Care in Action: Rowena's Story 197
Energy Management 199
Self-Actualisation 200
Final Thoughts 202
Key Insights 202
Action Steps 204

CHAPTER 9: THE PATH FORWARD **205**

The Story of the Earth School 205
The CLEAR Coaching Model: A Framework for Continued Growth 207
The Five Elements of the CLEAR Model of Coaching 210
Next Steps 212
Final Words 214

ABOUT THE AUTHOR **217**

FURTHER READING **219**

WANT MORE? **221**

Testimonials

" Working with Mandy over the past six months has been transformative. Her ability to quickly identify core issues and provide tailored strategies helped me develop a more resilient mindset and deep self-awareness. Mandy's holistic approach goes beyond surface goals. She helped me shift limiting beliefs, gain clarity on my purpose, and grow in every area of life. Her insight, support, and structured guidance truly set her apart. I now have tools that will serve me well beyond coaching. I highly recommend her to anyone ready to unlock their full potential."

— DIRK VON PLESSEN,
  PROJECT DIRECTOR

" The transformation I experienced while working with Mandy has been nothing short of amazing. For years, I dabbled in self-development on my own. I understood the concepts, but lacked the tools, strategies, and accountability to truly move forward. When I hit rock bottom, I decided enough was enough, and committed to working with Mandy. That decision changed everything. My advice to others is — don't wait until things fall apart to start this work. Mandy's coaching helps you tap into your full potential and show up each day as the best version of yourself. The transformation I received working with Mandy inspired me to undertake my own training and certification to become a life coach. During my certification training it was asked who had undergone coaching themselves — I proudly detailed my remarkable journey through my coaching with Mandy. I now have a High-Performance Mindset, and I'm grateful every day that I chose to invest in myself."

— TINA BOSS,
  SOUL ALIGNMENT & BREATHWORK GUIDE

" I just wanted to give a massive shoutout to Mandy Napier from Mindset for Success for the exceptional coaching she continues to provide me. Having worked with world-class coaches as part of the Platinum Group with Tony Robbins, and learning directly from thought leaders like Robert Kiyosaki and Jay Abraham, I hold incredibly high standards when it comes to personal development. Yet, Mandy's coaching has consistently stood out. I've been working with Mandy for several years now, and that long-term consistency has been a game-changer. There's immense value in having someone who truly knows you — your strengths, blind spots, growth goals, and even your patterns. That depth of understanding allows Mandy to challenge me at just the right times, hold me to a higher standard, and help me create lasting transformation. Her guidance has created a powerful ripple effect across both my personal and professional life. I'm clearer, more grounded, and more aligned with my vision than ever before. If you're serious about growth and want a coach who's not only skilled but deeply committed to your success, I can't recommend Mandy highly enough."

— SHANE ANDERSON,
PRESIDENT HIGH PEEK PRO

" When I reconnected with Mandy, I was at rock bottom: struggling with CPTSD, anxiety, and depression. Traditional approaches weren't working, but Mandy's holistic mindset coaching offered something radically different. Her unwavering support, practical tools, and deep understanding helped me shift my thinking, grow in self-confidence, and silence my inner critic. Through one-on-one coaching and the Unshakeable Confidence group, I've become more present, self-compassionate, and aligned with my values. I even had the confidence to apply for, and land, a role I never imagined possible. Mandy's work is life changing. Her knowledge, warmth, and dedication are truly extraordinary."

— SELENA BLACK

" I first came to Mandy over 12 years ago, initially to focus on getting my health on track. But not long after, my work life began to spiral. I had stepped into a leadership role that felt completely beyond my skill level, and the stress was overwhelming. My confidence dropped, my health suffered, and I felt stuck.

Working with Mandy gave me tools and insights that changed everything. I started to understand how I process, think, and lead. We created action plans that helped me build confidence, develop my leadership style, and, most importantly, reconnect with myself. I learned that I didn't have to be owned by my job, and I didn't have to keep proving myself.

Eventually, I found the courage to leave a toxic environment, take a dream trip around the world for 11 months, and came back to a whole new chapter. I gained a Masters in Leadership and moved to another company, recently gaining a promotion.

The self-awareness I've gained is the greatest gift. I've grown, stretched, let go of old patterns, and most importantly, realised my value and the importance of self-care. I continue to evolve and redefine my limits. Coaching with Mandy has been one of the most empowering investments I've made in myself.

— ROWENA PALLISTER,
  EXPLORATION AND MINING PROFESSIONAL

" Mandy is exceptional at what she does. Her coaching is both a talent and a skill that I've deeply appreciated, and it's had a significant impact on my life. Mandy's techniques are vast, and she always has another approach to try, delivered with grace, curiosity and empathy. I still credit much of my success in landing (and keeping) a role I couldn't have even imagined before our work together. I wouldn't hesitate to recommend Mandy, and I anticipate that I will be a returning client when I am ready to continue."

— LORI CLARK

" Mandy's wealth of knowledge and experience combined with her business 'Mindset for Success' is next level. Her coaching has helped me achieve beyond the norm, elevate my confidence, and maintain continued excellence. Limiting beliefs have been challenged and my vision propelled forward. I have practical tools for unlocking both personal and professional growth. It's a brilliant training ground for anyone committed to achieving their very best in all spheres of life."

— ANGELA HARRISON,
GENERAL MANAGER (CANBERRA), ENGINEERS AUSTRALIA

" Before working with Mandy, I had big goals but felt stuck and unsure how to get going. Since starting, I've got unstuck and into massive action — creating amazing results and opening the door to exciting new possibilities. I highly recommend Mandy Napier and Mindset for Success. She shares her wealth of experience and knowledge with inspiration and encouragement. Using her skillset, she helps you clarify your vision and achieve what's truly possible!"

— CAROLYN GRESIK,
SINGER, PERFORMER

" I had the pleasure of working with Mandy to help improve not only my mindset around success but also the business development for my gym in Warana. I couldn't have hoped for a better outcome over the 12 weeks, and the results are evident in the continued success of the business. Mandy helped me understand myself on a deeper level, particularly around my blockages, while also guiding me through business strategy. She methodically broke down my daily non-negotiables, helping me stay focused on my overarching goal instead of getting caught up in being 'busy. I'd happily recommend working with Mandy. You won't regret it."

— OLIVER COLE, OWNER,
THE KAIZEN MOVEMENT

" I don't even know if there are words enough to express the gratitude I have for the kindness and help Mandy has shown me. She supported me through a very dark period of my life and patiently worked with me, giving me the tools and help I needed to dig my way out. She stuck with me and supported me the entire way through. I've learned so much. Most of us can't see our own shadows or identify our habitual patterns, but Mandy helps you to find them, see where they came from and then walks you through the steps to clear and transform them. I cannot recommend Mandy enough. If you're looking to uncover your blockages and move forward, whether in life or business, Mandy can help. Thank you so much for everything."

— HUNTER CAVANAGH

" Working with Mandy as my coach has enabled me to achieve more than I ever thought was possible. Mandy is always professional, encouraging, and supportive. I cannot speak highly enough of her as both an expert in her field and as a generous human being. Mandy has a unique ability to provide exactly the strategy that will work for you. She can share her deep level of expertise in a simple yet highly effective way. Thanks to her guidance, I was finally able to create and launch the projects and my podcast, Powered by Mind, which I had been stuck on for years. I would wholeheartedly recommend Mandy to anyone looking to reach their full potential. Thank you, Mandy, for everything you have done for me. I'm incredibly appreciative!"

— JO AULD,
  CONNECTED KNOWLEDGE OFFICER

" Mandy has provided me with guidance and practical tools to upgrade my mindset to improve my confidence, better value my worth, and step into my power. I really look forward to our conversations and her next gem of advice to improve further."

— CLAIRE STEVENS,
SURGEON AND ADVENTURER

"I highly recommend Mandy to anyone seeking to grow and expand their mindset. Mandy is an expert in her field. She is very intuitive and can reveal insights into what is holding you back from your greatness. Her courses are practical, hands on and teach you skills for life that you can use in all aspects of your life. I have gained new insights & perspectives and added new tools to my kitbag for conquering life's challenges and enjoying life."

— REBECCA WATT,
FOREIGN EXCHANGE, ADVICE RISK/COMPLIANCE,
FINANCIAL ADVICE

"Mandy recently spoke at one of our Women with Influence monthly community events. Considering the challenges we were heading into, she gave us a great perspective around what we as female corporate consultants can do to self-manage, set habits and routines and create self-care to get through tough times. She also talked about the power of celebration and connection to grow through uncertainty. Thank you so much for your generous contribution to our community Mandy, I know the ladies got so much for your incredible experience and insights."

— JANE ANDERSON,
GROWTH STRATEGIST FOR FEMALE CONSULTANTS

"Before I worked with Mandy, I was in a dark place; stuck, defeated, and ready to give up. I'd tried everything: therapy, books, workshops, but nothing created lasting change. Working with Mandy was a turning point. She helped me recognise how my automatic negative thinking was sabotaging my progress and showed me how to rewire those patterns. I now have clarity, direction, and real tools to shift my mindset and take charge of my life. I'm no longer stuck. I'm moving forward with optimism and purpose. If you feel like you're living the same struggle on repeat, Mandy is the breakthrough you've been looking for."

— SHIRLEY JONES

Foreword

Mandy Napier is a former Ironman age group athlete who represented Australia in triathlons and competed in the prestigious Hawaiian Ironman World Championships.

While many people focus on the events and outcomes, what makes athletes exceptional is their mindset, discipline in training, and the ability to push beyond both real and perceived limitations to cross the line.

As humans, we're naturally curious about what is possible and want to live up to our potential. It's also no secret that being a high performer provides personal and professional benefits, but in pursuit of this, there's often a dark side.

High performers by nature aim for mastery, but are incredibly hard on themselves, and can struggle to find balance between striving to be the best version of themselves and being kind when the goals they work so hard for don't go to plan.

Mandy is a world-class thought leader, educator, and mindset coach who respects this tension and knows how to harness it for exceptional results.

With deep and significant experience in what it takes to be a champion, not just in sport but in life, Mandy continues to live and breathe what she's learned over the years to help her clients achieve sustainable, healthy high performance.

Rewire is the book for anyone who holds themselves to a high standard and wants to live a connected and purposeful life on their terms.

The wisdom shared in Rewire provides practical tools and the space to better understand yourself at a deeper level, cultivate a high-performance mindset, and take intentional, consistent action — ultimately, to be your best and create a lasting impact in the world.

MELANIE MARSHALL
TEAM PERFORMANCE SPECIALIST,
FOUNDER OF ADAPT & EXCEL

Introduction

*"The world exists as you perceive it.
It is not what you see, it is how you see it.
It is not what you hear, but how you hear it."*

— RUMI

This timeless wisdom reminds us that our perception shapes our reality. We often assume the world is fixed and that our circumstances define us. But the truth, as Rumi's insight reveals, is far more empowering. When we shift how we see and interpret the world, our experiences — and ultimately, our lives, are transformed.

This idea is the foundation of this book, *REWIRE*.

Much like adjusting the lens of a camera, a simple shift in perspective can bring clarity and reveal hidden opportunities you may never have noticed.

By learning to change the way you think, respond, and show up, you can train your mind, rewire your brain, and take control of your life. When you work from the inside out, you can transform your outer world too.

THE POWER OF PERSPECTIVE

> *"When you change the way you look at things, the things you look at change."*
>
> — WAYNE DYER

Viktor Frankl, a Holocaust survivor and author of *Man's Search for Meaning*, endured unimaginable suffering in Nazi concentration camps. He lost his family, his freedom, and he even nearly lost his life. Yet, amidst all this darkness, he made a powerful choice, one that no one could take from him. He chose to control his mind. By doing so, he maintained his inner freedom and sense of purpose, even in the face of extreme suffering.

While he couldn't change his circumstances, he could control his response to them. He embraced specific mental strategies to endure gruelling hardships and maintain a positive meaning in his circumstances. Already a practicing and successful psychiatrist, his career was cut short by the Nazi annexation of his homeland Austria in 1938. In 1942 he was deported with his family to the Theresienstadt concentration camp, where he survived the daily horror by using visualisation techniques to imagine himself giving psychotherapy lectures after his release, which provided him with purpose and hope during incredibly tough times.

When the war was almost over, his family was transferred to Auschwitz, where his mother, brother and wife were killed or died of disease. After miraculously surviving this gruesome ordeal, after Austria was liberated, he returned to his psychiatry career, where he went on to work at Austrian hospitals and universities and became the founder of the third school of Viennese Psychotherapy — the Logotherapy School.

Today, mental rehearsal and visualisation are powerful tools that athletes embrace to help them gain an edge in their sport.

Moreover, Frankl discovered deep significance in the small, unexpected moments of life. When he was stripped of his possessions, he discovered a page from a Hebrew prayer book in the pocket of his new prison uniform.

This unexpected discovery strengthened his commitment to living out his faith through action, offering encouragement to fellow prisoners, maintaining inner strength, and finding purpose in even the smallest moments of kindness and reflection.

His ability to reframe his experience not only helped him endure but allowed him to thrive after the war, developing his groundbreaking philosophy on the power of mindset.

We may not control what happens to us, but we do have the power to control how we respond.

THE MODERN STRUGGLE

Today, while most of us living in Western countries aren't facing the same extreme circumstances as Frankl, many people feel trapped, stuck in stress, uncertainty, and self-doubt. And it's not just since the pandemic. Way before this, I believe people were struggling to find meaning in their lives and align their actions with their dreams.

In 2013, a survey of 12,000 professionals by Harvard Business Review, found that about 50% of those surveyed felt their jobs had no meaning or significance.

Furthermore, the 2024 State of the Global Workplace Report reveals that disengaged employees account for $8.9 trillion in lost productivity globally.

Today, despite having more opportunities, resources, and digital connectivity than ever before, studies show that people are feeling more overwhelmed and disconnected. Loneliness has been declared an epidemic, which has dire consequences on our wellbeing and happiness. According to Noreena Hertz, author of the book *The Lonely Century*, loneliness now has the same impact on health as smoking fifteen cigarettes a day.

This highlights that while external pressures exist, it is often our internal barriers that hold us back the most. If one man can thrive amidst the horrors of a concentration camp, surely, on a global level, we shouldn't be feeling so lonely, disengaged, and disconnected? Yet, it seems we are.

Take Peter, a successful entrepreneur and father of two. On the surface, he had everything: an expanding business, a strong network, and a loving family. Yet, when he came to me, he confessed, *"Despite everything I've built, I feel like I am doing this alone."* Through our work together, I helped him uncover some old patterns and beliefs. One of which, a relentless drive to succeed, something he had picked up from his father, had unintentionally created isolation.

When he realised the source of his problems, and we worked together to shift his internal dialogue, creating better habits of thought, he began to shift his mindset. Shortly after working together, he said he felt more connected with himself, which strengthened his relationships as he reconnected with what truly mattered.

Like Peter, many high achievers operate on autopilot, believing that success means *doing more*. Success requires more than hard work; it involves self-discovery, getting to know yourself deeply, identifying limiting patterns and habits, clarifying your goals, making the appropriate changes to your thinking, rewriting your narrative, and following through with aligned actions.

The Shift That Changes Everything

True transformation begins within. Your thoughts, emotions, and actions are energy, and they shape both your inner world and your external reality.

Emerging neuroscience confirms what ancient wisdom has long known: your mindset determines your potential.

Dr. Joe Dispenza highlights this in *Breaking the Habit of Being Yourself*, stating:

*"To change is to think greater than how we feel.
To change is to act greater than the familiar
feelings of the memorized self."*

This means real change isn't just about setting goals or working harder; it's about reprogramming the way you think, behave, and respond so that success becomes your default.

THE PATH TO A HIGH-PERFORMANCE MINDSET

REWIRE is about applying knowledge to create transformations. Developing a high-performance mindset starts with awareness and intentional action. This book will help you cultivate the clarity to know what truly matters, the consistency to take purposeful steps every day, and the impact to create meaningful change in both your personal and professional lives.

- **Clarity**:
  To achieve excellence, you must first understand what truly matters. You will discover tools to help you create a compelling future, set clear goals that align with your values, and develop self-awareness from the inside out to ensure you are heading in the right direction.

- **Consistency**:
  Success is built on daily habits, not motivation. You'll learn how to establish empowering routines, develop mental and emotional strategies, and take purposeful action to ensure steady progress.

- **Impact**:
  True success isn't just about personal achievement; it's about who you become and how you manage your energy to influence and impact your life and the lives of those around you. By mastering your mindset, you'll unlock greater influence, leadership, and fulfillment.

All of this is achieved by making small, intentional shifts consistently, leading to powerful results over time.

Awareness is the first step to transformation.
Take a moment to reflect on where you are today by answering the following questions:

Do you have a clear vision for your life and goals?

....

Are your values aligned with your decisions and actions?

....

Do you take consistent action toward your goals?

....

Is your self-talk predominantly positive?

....

Do you know how to manage your emotional state effectively?

....

Do you feel like your life has purpose and meaning?

....

Are you great at staying focused, or do you often get distracted?

....

This isn't about judgement; it's about self-discovery, and a starting point to help you pinpoint exactly where to start first.

If you'd like to take a comprehensive self-assessment, you can access it in the REWIRE Resources portal, via the link or by using the QR code below.

https://bit.ly/3RmsIke

Use this tool to gain clarity on what's working, what needs attention, and where to focus your energy. As you work through the book, you can revisit these insights, track your progress, and refine your approach. You will also find additional tools and resources in the portal that I have referenced throughout the book, each designed to support your journey.

Keep in mind that true transformation is a gradual process, not an instantaneous event. It's small, consistent shifts that reshape your mindset, strengthen your core energy, and create powerful, lasting results. Self-awareness is the foundation of transformation. Now, let's explore what a high-performance mindset truly is and why it matters, laying the foundation for everything that follows.

CHAPTER 1:
What is a High-Performance Mindset?

*"Champions aren't made in gyms.
Champions are made from something they have
deep inside of them;
a desire, a dream, a vision."*

— MUHAMMAD ALI

DEFINING A HIGH-PERFORMANCE MINDSET

What does it mean to have a high-performance mindset? At its core, it is a way of thinking and operating that enables individuals to consistently perform at their best, whether in business, sports, relationships, or personal goals. This mindset isn't exclusive to elite athletes or CEOs, you can cultivate it too.

A high-performance mindset is the invisible edge that distinguishes those who consistently achieve extraordinary results. These individuals have learned to manage their thoughts and emotions, align their actions with their values, and consistently pursue their goals. They master mental skills that keep them focused, resilient, and adaptable, even in the face of challenges. At its core, this mindset is shaped by three things:

Clarity: Knowing who you are, what drives you, and what truly matters.

Consistency: Taking daily, intentional action to build and sustain momentum.

Impact: Using your mindset, skills, and strengths to create meaningful change in your life and the lives of others.

THE POWER OF CONTROLLING THE CONTROLLABLES — CRAIG TILEY'S STORY

*"What I learned is to let go of
the things you can't control.
Control the controllables.
Don't worry or get worked up
about the things you can't control.
But the things you do have control over,
just do your best."*

— CRAIG TILEY

As the CEO of Tennis Australia, Craig Tiley faced an unprecedented challenge during the 2022 Australian Open, one of the nation's most prestigious and globally recognised sporting events.

First, shifting government policies due to pandemic restrictions created constant uncertainty and discontent among the Victorian people.

Then came the global controversy surrounding Novak Djokovic's deportation, followed by public outrage in Victoria. Many residents had endured months of strict lockdowns, yet international players were allowed to travel and compete; by many it was seen as unfair. The pressure on Tiley was immense, and many people doubted if he could pull it off. Yet, Tiley focused on what he could control. Despite global scrutiny and challenges, he successfully delivered a world-class event.

Tiley showed focus and resilience, successfully ensuring the tournament went ahead despite external challenges. The following year, the Australian Open broke attendance records, illustrating that staying clear on your purpose, consistency in navigating challenges, and unwavering determination can lead to extraordinary results and a lasting impact.

The Australian Open has firmly established itself as one of the premiere tennis Grand Slam tournaments globally. In 2025, the event set a new attendance record, with over 1.2 million spectators attending over three weeks.

Tiley's story is a powerful reminder that mindset is your greatest asset, and self-belief and unwavering determination are your strongest allies. When external factors threaten to derail you, refocus on what you can control: your thoughts, emotions, actions, and choices.

THE KEY TRAITS OF A HIGH-PERFORMANCE MINDSET

1. Curiosity and Passion

High performers are lifelong learners who embrace curiosity and challenge assumptions. Their passion fuels perseverance, helping them push through setbacks and find the inner strength to keep going when others would quit.

Take Claire, a client of mine who reached out to me in 2023 while navigating the challenges of a new position and setting up a private surgical practice. She balances her demanding medical career with solo ultra-endurance races across remote terrain. Through our work together, she learned how to structure her schedule in a way that allowed her to juggle her passions, honour her adventurous spirit, and maintain professional excellence.

Her recent achievement was finishing as one of the top female competitors in the Silk Road Mountain Race; an unsupported, single-stage endurance event through the rugged mountains of Kyrgyzstan. Even more incredibly, Claire had never trained or competed at high altitude before, which made her accomplishment all the more remarkable.

You can indeed have it all, with the right mindset and strategies.

2. Focus

Distractions are everywhere, but high performers train their minds to ignore distractions and stay focused on their goals and what truly matters.

Take Simone Biles, the most decorated gymnast in history. During competitions, she must block out the noise of the crowd, the pressure of expectations, and even her own nerves to execute routines with precision. A single lapse in focus could mean the difference between victory and failure, or even serious injury.

At the Tokyo 2020 Olympics, Biles experienced the 'twisties'; a dangerous mental block where a gymnast loses awareness of their body in the air. Recognising that she could no longer perform safely, she made the courageous decision to withdraw from multiple events. This wasn't a sign of weakness but of deep self-awareness. She knew that without full mental clarity and focus, pushing through could have resulted in serious harm. When she eventually returned to competition, she had regained her confidence and composure, proving that true high performers understand when to step back, reset, and refocus.

Her ability to maintain laser-sharp focus, particularly during high-stakes moments, has been a key factor in her dominance in the sport.

3. Grit: The Power of Self-Belief and Perseverance

I often use the word "grit" because it captures the essence of self-belief and perseverance: the ability to act despite fear and to overcome challenges.

Psychologist Angela Duckworth defines grit as a relentless perseverance toward long-term goals. At its core lies self-belief, the unwavering conviction that you are capable of more than you once thought possible. Self-belief is the fuel that keeps you moving forward, even when obstacles seem insurmountable.

This mindset is what enabled Roger Bannister to break the four-minute mile and Eliud Kipchoge to run a sub-two-hour marathon. Kipchoge's famous mantra, "No human is limited," was born from his deep self-belief. He knew he could break the barrier long before he physically did. What we believe about ourselves and our abilities directly determines what we can achieve.

4. Emotional Mastery

Top performers maintain control over their emotions and refuse to allow their feelings to dictate their actions. They learn how to manage stress, setbacks, and pressure, allowing them to stay composed and focused on their path. Success and excellence are not a matter of chance; they are built through mindset, discipline, and deliberate, purposeful, and strategic actions every day, whether you feel like it or not.

5. Continual Growth

High performers embrace feedback and see failure as an opportunity to grow. Moreover, they constantly refine their approach, seek out new and better ways of achieving their results, and are committed to lifelong learning.

6. Energy Management

We are energy beings, not machines, and great performances require a massive amount of energy. The best performers know when to push hard and when to step back and recover. They prioritise movement, nutrition, sleep, and mental strategies like mindfulness or meditation to maintain sustainable peak performance over the long term.

7. Incremental Improvements

Small, incremental changes, what former Welsh cycling coach Sir David Brailsford calls marginal gains, can lead to extraordinary results over time.

Brailsford revolutionised British cycling and Team Sky by focusing on every possible performance factor, from optimising bike mechanics and aerodynamics to refining nutrition, sleep quality, and even ensuring proper hand hygiene to prevent illness. His philosophy was simple: if you improve just 1% in multiple areas, the cumulative effect will create massive success.

Under his leadership, Team Sky dominated world cycling, winning the Tour de France multiple times. In 2012, his marginal gains approach extended beyond cycling when he applied it to Team GB's Olympic squad, helping them achieve unprecedented success at the London Games. His groundbreaking methods earned him a knighthood for his contributions to British cycling, recognising his role in transforming the sport and proving that small, consistent improvements compound into game-changing results.

This principle isn't just for elite athletes; it applies to business, leadership, and personal success. Every action you take, no matter how small, moves you forward when you are clear on what you want and why it matters.

FINAL THOUGHTS

You may be wondering, *"Can I truly develop these traits and make a difference in my life or the world?"* The answer is yes. Change starts with individuals, and research indicates that small, purposeful actions compound into extraordinary results, just like money grows with consistent investment over time.

Consider an experiment conducted in the 1960s. Maharishi Mahesh Yogi proposed that a small group practicing transcendental meditation could influence societal change. Known as the Maharishi Effect, research showed that when just 1% of a population engaged in meditation, crime rates decreased, and overall well-being improved. This principle highlights the ripple effect of focused, collective effort, and it starts with one person.

KEY INSIGHTS

- **Controlling the controllables:**
  Focus on what you can change and let go of what you can't.

- **Your mindset determines your limits:**
  Athletes and leaders have redefined what's possible. You are far more powerful than you think you are.

- **Small, daily improvements lead to lasting success:**
  Consistent effort and small steps build momentum and lead to extraordinary results.

Finally, remember, a high-performance mindset isn't something you're born with; it's something you can cultivate. Through clarity, intentional effort, consistency, and determination, you shape your mindset, transform your results, and inspire those around you.

In the next chapter, we'll discuss the importance of cultivating a high-performance mindset in today's fast-changing world.

CHAPTER 2:
Why a High-Performance Mindset Is Critical Today

"We cannot become what we need by remaining what we are."

— JOHN MAXWELL

THE DEMANDS OF MODERN LIFE

In today's fast-paced and unpredictable world, cultivating a high-performance mindset is no longer a luxury, it's a necessity. Rapid societal shifts, technological disruption, economic challenges, and workplace instability have left many people feeling deflated and searching for purpose.

These challenges demand resilience, adaptability, and focus. Without the right mindset, it's easy to feel overwhelmed or stuck. The pandemic served as a wake-up call, exposing vulnerabilities in how we approach work, relationships, and personal growth. Some individuals experienced a "mindset awakening," re-evaluating their values and priorities. Others struggled with isolation, uncertainty, and unprecedented stress.

Whether you're leading a team, pursuing personal goals, or seeking more balance in your life, developing a high-performance mindset is key to thriving in today's reality.

WHY CHANGE IS URGENT

1. A Crisis of Trust

The 2022 Edelman Trust Barometer declared we have entered a "Cycle of Distrust." Institutions, once seen as pillars of stability, are viewed with growing scepticism. Even in workplaces, trust remains fragile. Paul Zak's research shows that higher levels of trust correlate with greater productivity, collaboration, and well-being. Yet trust must be earned, requiring leaders to align their actions with their words.

2. Mental Well-Being in Decline

We know from Gallup's 2024 State of the Global Workplace Report that stress, sadness, anxiety, and anger have peaked in our society. Trillions of dollars are lost in productivity and revenue.

3. A Lack of Connection and Meaning

Despite digital connectivity, meaningful relationships have declined. The Harvard Study of Adult Development, one of the longest-running studies on well-being, has found that strong relationships are the key to happiness, longevity, and better mental and physical health. Abraham Maslow's hierarchy of needs also highlights connection as a fundamental human necessity, yet many feel isolated or unfulfilled in their work and personal lives.

WHY A HIGH-PERFORMANCE MINDSET IS THE ANSWER

These challenges underscore why developing a high-performance mindset is essential. This mindset equips individuals to:

- Build resilience in the face of uncertainty.
- Reclaim focus in a world full of distractions.
- Rediscover purpose and meaning in their lives and work.
- Foster trust and meaningful connections with others.

FROM DEFLATED TO ENERGISED

When Sarah, a senior executive in the finance industry, first came to me, she was feeling deflated. The demands of her role had drained her energy, and she felt stuck in a cycle of overwhelm and frustration. Despite her past success, she lacked clarity on her next steps and felt disengaged from both her work and personal life.

At first, she struggled with scattered focus, wanting change but not knowing how to move forward. We worked on identifying her core values and priorities, helping her shift from a reactive mindset to one of intentional action.

Over time, she gained clarity, prioritised what truly mattered, and developed consistent habits that aligned with her vision. She learned to manage her energy rather than just her time, setting clear boundaries and focusing on impactful work.

Within months, Sarah moved from frustration to confidence, and eventually to a state of energised performance, where she felt in control, fulfilled, and empowered. She didn't just improve her productivity; she transformed the way she approached her career and life.

THE HIGH-PERFORMANCE MINDSET VALUE MODEL

Chances are, you're not training for the Olympics, attempting to run a marathon in under two hours, or cycling solo across the Silk Road. But make no mistake, your performance matters.

Each day, you perform in various aspects of life: work, relationships, business, health, and self-leadership. Some performances are big and obvious, like pitching to an investor, presenting a major project, or sitting an important exam. Others seem small, like how you start your morning, the conversations you have, or the way you handle unexpected challenges. Yet, each one plays a role in shaping your results.

One thing is constant: your internal state, your thoughts, emotions, energy, and focus, directly impact how well you perform.

As Michael Phelps, one of the greatest Olympians of all time, put it:

> *"I can only control my performance.
> If I do my best, then I can feel good at the end
> of the day."*

And that's exactly what high performance is about, learning to take charge of what you can control so you can show up as your best self, more often.

UNDERSTANDING THE VALUE MODEL

Before diving into how to elevate your performance, let's first understand where you are today. The VALUE Model below, is a roadmap that helps you assess your current state, so you can determine the next step toward greater clarity, consistency, and impact.

Each level of the model reflects a combination of your internal state (thoughts, emotions, energy) and your external focus (where you direct your attention and effort). As you move up the model, you gain more control, alignment, and momentum.

One thing is certain, staying stuck at the lower levels comes at a cost. Poor performances lead to stress, wasted time, lost opportunities, and diminished confidence. But by actively working on yourself, you shift into higher levels of clarity, energy, and effectiveness.

THE SIX LEVELS OF THE VALUE MODEL

	STATE	FOCUS	PERFORMANCE
6	Energised	IMPACT	90% - 100%
5	Confident	CONSISTENCY	70% - 90%
4	Prioritised	ACTION	50% - 70%
3	Overwhelmed	CLARITY	30% - 50%
2	Frustrated	PLANNING	10% - 30%
1	Deflated	DECISION	0% - 10%

Level 1: DEFLATED

State:
Low energy, lack of motivation. Fear, doubt, and stagnation dominate.

Focus:
Negative: dwelling on uncertainty, stuck in hesitation.

Performance:
Minimal progress; procrastination and avoidance.

At this level, you feel flat, stuck, or exhausted. Too much change, uncertainty, or repetition has drained your motivation, leaving you feeling directionless. This was common during the pandemic when many people went into survival mode, unsure of their next step.

> **Solution:**
> The first step to moving forward?
> *Making a decision.*
> Decide that staying here isn't serving you and commit to even the smallest step forward.

Level 2: FRUSTRATED

State:
Restless, aware of wasted time and energy, but lacking clarity.

Focus:
Scattered, on too many possibilities without alignment.

Performance:
Some action, but inconsistent and ineffective.

Frustration kicks in when you realise you want more but aren't sure how to get there. You may feel like you're spinning your wheels, putting in effort but seeing little progress.

Solution:
To move beyond this stage, you need a plan.
Get clear on where you want to go and what truly matters.
Planning is key.

Level 3: OVERWHELMED

State:
Stress and confusion dominate. Too many options lead to paralysis.

Focus:
Unclear, overthinking, struggling to decide what to tackle first.

Performance:
Lots of effort, little progress. One step forward, two steps back.

At this level, your mind feels crowded, and it's easy to fall into analysis paralysis. You know action is needed, but where do you even start?

Solution:
Ask better questions:
- *"What's the one most important thing I can do right now?"*
- *"If I could only focus on three things this week, what would they be?"*

Curiosity is a powerful energy.
Asking the right questions shifts your focus from overwhelm to clarity, allowing you to regain control.

Level 4: PRIORITISED

State:
Clarity begins to form. A sense of direction emerges.

Focus:
Intentional, on high-impact actions that move the needle.

Performance:
Progress speeds up and momentum builds.

At this level, you're no longer reacting, you're choosing. You've identified what truly matters, and you're acting on it. As Stephen Covey wisely said: "Put first things first."

> **Solution:**
> Action is the antidote to doubt.
> Taking small, intentional steps builds self-trust and sets you up for the next level.

Level 5: CONFIDENT

State:
Self-belief strengthens. Greater alignment between thoughts, emotions, and actions.

Focus:
Purposeful: on growth, long-term success, and contribution.

Performance:
Consistent, reliable, high-quality outcomes.

Confidence doesn't come from waiting until you feel ready. It comes from proving to yourself that you can do hard things.

> **Solution:**
> At this stage, consistency is key.
> You show up, follow through, and trust yourself — even when challenges arise.

Level 6: ENERGISED

State:
High energy, mental clarity, and emotional stability.

Focus:
Big-picture thinking — sustained growth, impact, and contribution.

Performance:
Peak flow state. Success feels natural and fulfilling.

At this level, momentum fuels itself. Your efforts compound, your energy is contagious, and you operate with clarity and ease.

Solution:
Here, you focus on prioritising your mental, emotional, and physical energy, because you understand that to perform at your best, you must first take care of yourself. High energy attracts high energy.
When you operate at this level, your influence and impact ripple far beyond just yourself.

WHERE DO YOU SIT?

This model isn't about judgement, it's about awareness. Recognising where you are is the first step to moving forward.

Which level resonates with you the most?

What's one shift you can make today to move up a level?

High performance isn't about perfection, it's about progress. Every small improvement you make compounds into powerful results over time.

What's Next?

Now that you understand the VALUE Model and have identified where you currently stand, it's time to explore what might be holding you back.

In the next chapter, we'll look at the obstacles to a high-performance mindset, uncover the rules of the mind, and explore how the two parts of your mind play a crucial role in shaping your results and success. Together, we'll uncover ways to break free from self-sabotaging patterns and unlock your full potential.

KEY INSIGHTS

✓ **Gaining clarity** on what you want and why is fundamental to progress.

✓ **Consistent action,** no matter how small, leads to success.

✓ **Managing your energy** is as important as, if not more important than, managing your time.

✓ **Your level of impact** is a reflection of your core energy, how you show up, think, and feel about yourself.

CHAPTER 3:
Barriers to a High-Performance Mindset

"We cannot become what we need by remaining what we are."

— JOHN MAXWELL

WHY DO WE HOLD OURSELVES BACK?

Despite having big goals and a desire to perform at their best, many people never reach their potential. The barriers we face aren't always external; more often, they stem from within. Our ingrained habits, beliefs, and subconscious patterns shape our mindset and influence our actions, often without us even realising it.

The first step to overcoming these barriers is awareness. Without recognising the unconscious rules that govern our thinking, we remain stuck in habit mode — autopilot, repeating old patterns. But once we become aware, we gain the power to challenge our patterns, rewire our responses, and shift our mindset to one that supports our success.

As Dr. Joe Dispenza explains:

> *"Neuroscience research proves that 95% of who you are by the age of 35 is a memorised set of behaviours, emotional reactions, unconscious habits, hard-wired attitudes, beliefs, and perceptions that function as a computer program."*

This is a vital point. It's why change can feel so difficult for many, and impossible for some. It's not about willpower, it's about rewiring deeply ingrained mental patterns. If we don't understand how our minds operate, or know how to change what isn't working, we risk falling back into old habits, or being driven by our old patterns, no matter how much we want to change. We fight, get frustrated, and often fail to succeed, despite all our efforts. This is why understanding the rules of the mind becomes essential.

THE RULES OF THE MIND

It's helpful to know that your mind isn't working against you; it's simply following innate, hard-wired rules designed to keep you safe and comfortable.

However, without awareness and knowledge, these rules can keep you stuck. By learning how your mind works, you can gain control over it instead of letting it control you.

As Buddha said:

*"Rule your mind,
or it will rule you."*

1. Your Mind Believes What You Tell It

*"Your beliefs become your thoughts,
Your thoughts become your words,
Your words become your actions,
Your actions become your habits,
Your habits become your values,
Your values become your destiny."*

— MAHATMA GANDHI

When you repeat thoughts frequently, they become habits, and then, your reality, or destiny. Moreover, as many of your thoughts are the same as the day before, they dictate your results. Whether you tell yourself, *"I'll never be good at this"* or *"I always find a way,"* your mind will seek evidence to prove you right. Mastering and managing your self-talk matters and is crucial to rewiring your brain and changing your results.

Take Sally for example. When she first came to work with me, she was constantly doubting herself and struggling with her confidence. Together, we uncovered key limiting beliefs and negative self-talk about herself that were holding her back. From there, we replaced the old beliefs with new empowering beliefs and created some positive statements (POSTs), such as, *"Every day I am becoming an even more capable and inspiring leader."* We literally rewrote her internal script.

At first, it felt unnatural, just like any new behaviour or strategy. But as she consistently reinforced these new thoughts, her mindset shifted. As she took action in alignment with her new beliefs, she grew in self-belief and confidence. Over time, this translated into stronger leadership and greater impact.

As Wayne Dyer said:

"When you change the way you look at things, the things you look at change."

2. Your Mind Seeks Comfort, Not Growth

Your brain is wired to avoid pain and discomfort and seek pleasure. Growth requires stepping outside your comfort zone, but your mind often resists by triggering fear or doubt, leading to procrastination.

This is why taking the first step is always the hardest. The mind magnifies challenges, turning small hurdles into seemingly insurmountable obstacles.

As Lao Tzu, philosopher and author of the Tao Te Ching, wisely said:

"A journey of a thousand miles begins with a single step."

Looking at the mountain you need to conquer feels daunting; however, when you take that first step, everything feels easier. That's why I have deep admiration for my clients who take the initiative to reach out. I know just how hard that first step can be.

3. Your Mind Is Wired for Habit

Most of our daily actions are driven by habit. Without awareness, we unconsciously repeat the same behaviours and patterns, often expecting different results. The mind seeks efficiency, so it defaults to what is familiar, even if it no longer serves us.

As Einstein famously said:

> *"Insanity is doing the same thing
> over and over again
> and expecting a different result."*

Later, we'll explore how consciously creating new habits forms the foundation for lasting change and high performance.

4. Your Mind Amplifies What You Focus On

Your mind works like a spotlight; whatever you focus on expands. If you focus on problems, you'll see more problems. If you focus on solutions, possibilities become clearer.

This is why it's vital to direct your thoughts intentionally. If you say, *"I don't want to be lazy,"* your subconscious doesn't recognise negatives. It only hears *"lazy."* It's actually just another way of saying you're lazy! Instead, reframe your focus: *"I am disciplined and take consistent action."*

5. Your Mind Has Two Parts: The Conscious and Subconscious

> *"Until you make the unconscious conscious,
> it will direct your life and you will call it fate."*
>
> — CARL JUNG

One of the biggest reasons people struggle with lasting change is that they don't realise the subconscious mind is running the show.

We consciously set goals, make plans for our future success, yet our subconscious is the storehouse of our memories, habits, unresolved emotions, past experiences, and deeply ingrained beliefs.

It is way more powerful, which means it usually wins. Remembering everything is energy, and the phrase, *'what we resist persists,'* is the key here. Fighting it with willpower alone rarely works.

Research by psychologist Dr. John Bargh suggests that up to 95% of our daily actions are driven by the subconscious mind.

In one well-known study, participants exposed to words related to ageing, such as 'Florida,' 'ageing,' 'walking stick' and 'wrinkle,' unknowingly walked more slowly when leaving the experiment.

This demonstrated how subconscious priming influences behaviour, often without our awareness. Even when we consciously want to change, these deep-seated programs often pull us back into operating in the same way.

Change doesn't happen at the conscious level alone. True transformation, along with learning, begins in the subconscious, which is why willpower alone is never enough. We must ensure our conscious goals align with our subconscious programs, which is rarely the case, or rewire the programs themselves.

COMMON BARRIERS TO A HIGH-PERFORMANCE MINDSET

Now that you understand the rules of the mind, let's look at the most common barriers that hold people back, and how to break free.

1. Fear of Failure

Mark, a project manager, struggled with presenting new ideas at work, fearing criticism and rejection. He knew he had a tendency to people-please and often found himself being swayed by more outspoken colleagues. This pattern left him feeling stuck and frustrated, causing him to miss valuable opportunities.

When he came to see me, he recognised the need to break this pattern. Together, we unpacked his fear of rejection, and reframed its meaning. With some new strategies, positive statements, and visualisation exercises, he gradually built confidence. As he began sharing his opinions more, he discovered they were well accepted and embraced. Over time, his contributions were recognised, and he earned a well-deserved promotion.

- **The Shift:**
  Unpack the fear behind failure, reframe it, and use it as a stepping stone, not a stop sign. Growth comes from stepping through fear and taking action.

2. The Negativity Bias

Our brains are hardwired to focus more on negative experiences than positive ones, which can lead to self-doubt, rumination, and overanalysing situations.

Take Susan, a senior executive who constantly replayed every minor mistake she made in meetings. Despite receiving positive feedback, she struggled to believe in herself and frequently doubted her abilities. I suggested she focus on three small wins each day, to train her brain to focus on progress rather than problems. As her self-belief grew, she added a gratitude practice, further strengthening her confidence, resilience, and overall sense of identity.

As psychologist Rick Hanson explains:

> *"The mind is like Velcro for negative experiences but Teflon for positive ones."*

- **The Shift:**
  Train your brain to focus on the positive by deliberately acknowledging your wins and strengths. Over time, this rewires your brain to make positivity a normal and natural default pattern.

3. Overachieving and The Need to Prove Oneself

High performers often struggle with the constant drive to achieve, operating in a perpetual state of being 'switched on' as they relentlessly pursue the next big project or goal.

Brett, a business owner, was caught in the cycle of *'achieve more, then I'll feel successful.'* When he identified that this belief stemmed from childhood, he realised he had been chasing success to fill an internal void. Through self-reflection and shifting his mindset, he began celebrating his progress rather than focusing on what was missing. This not only improved his self-belief and wellbeing, but also helped him grow his business with greater ease.

As Dan Sullivan explains in *The Gap and The Gain*, many high performers stay stuck in 'the gap', measuring success against an ever-moving target, rather than acknowledging how far they've come. Brett realised he had been doing exactly that, always chasing the next milestone. When I taught him to reflect on his progress at the end of each day, live in the 'gain', and celebrate his wins, he not only began to appreciate how far he had come but also developed a powerful habit of recognising his achievements. This small but profound shift significantly reduced his stress. Instead of constantly being 'on', he learned to balance his drive with appreciation and a deeper sense of fulfilment.

- **The Shift:**
  Success isn't just about pushing harder; it's about appreciating what you have, and knowing when to step back or push forward.

4. Over-Responsibility and People-Pleasing

Many professionals feel overly responsible for others, whether it's their staff, family, or clients. This often leads to burnout, resentment, and being stretched too thin.

Years ago, I fell into this trap, taking on too much responsibility for my team. I carried this burden without realising it was an unconscious pattern shaping my actions. It wasn't until I learned how deeply ingrained beliefs drive behaviour that I understood why I had been operating this way. This insight became a powerful turning point, not just in prioritising my own goals, like finally training for and competing in an Ironman triathlon, but also for the work I do today, helping others break free from their redundant and limiting programs.

- **The Shift:**
  Supporting others is important, but not at the expense of yourself. Remember, you can't pour from an empty cup. Prioritise yourself first.

5. Perfectionism

Perfectionism is often driven by a fear of getting something wrong, as well as by childhood experiences. Procrastination and anxiety are a result of this, as people worry about trying to control every aspect of their lives. For some people, this can manifest in panic attacks. When Zara came to work with me, she had struggled with anxiety all her life, experiencing occasional panic attacks that affected her sense of control.

A high achiever by nature, she set high standards for herself, but her fear of making mistakes held her back. One of her biggest goals was to start a family, and she realised that overcoming this challenge was essential to her future.

Through our work together, she applied key techniques to manage her anxiety, shift her mindset, and take back control. Over time, she became calmer, eliminated panic attacks altogether, and gained greater control over her life. Today, she is a happy mother to a young boy and continues to thrive while working part-time.

- **The Shift:**
  Work on getting to the core of what drives your perfectionism. Then, focus on breaking things into small steps, taking small, consistent action rather than waiting for the "perfect" moment. Show yourself kindness by recognising your accomplishments and appreciating what you have done instead of focusing on what you haven't achieved.

6. Ignoring You Are an Energy Being Who Cannot Go Forever

It's common for people to focus on managing time instead of managing energy. Most people have no idea they can't keep operating like a Duracell battery. However, we must replenish our mental and physical energy to sustain high performance.

We are not machines, we are energy beings. Tony Schwartz, author of *The Power of Full Engagement*, states:

*"Because energy capacity diminishes both
with overuse and underuse,
we must balance energy expenditure
with intermittent energy renewal."*

Dani, a driven entrepreneur, used to push herself to exhaustion, believing that working harder would lead to greater success. It wasn't until she prioritised sleep, recovery breaks, and exercise that she noticed a dramatic shift in her productivity. By working *with* her energy rather than against it, she achieved more in less time, without burning out.

- **The Shift:**
  Implement small but consistent energy-management habits, such as breathing techniques, hydration, movement, and recovery breaks, to sustain long-term performance.

7. The Power of Our Subconscious Beliefs and Redundant Patterns

One of the biggest obstacles to success is the power of limiting beliefs and deeply ingrained past programs.

Take Carol, a successful real estate agent with over 30 years' experience. Despite her expertise, she struggled to break into the million-dollar housing market, but couldn't pinpoint why. Through our work together, we uncovered a deep-seated belief she had carried since childhood, the belief that she wasn't 'good enough' for high-end sales. Once we cleared this limiting belief and replaced it with an empowering one, everything changed. She soon secured her first million-dollar sale. Just like Roger Bannister breaking the four-minute mile, once she proved it was possible, she continued to achieve many more, never looking back.

- **The Shift:**
  Identify limiting beliefs and actively replace them with empowering ones.

FINAL THOUGHTS

Breaking through mindset barriers is not about eliminating challenges, it's about recognising them and consciously choosing a different path. Awareness is the first step to change.

In Chapter 2, The VALUE Model provided a framework for assessing where you are today. This chapter explored the common barriers that may be keeping you stuck, whether it's frustration, perfectionism, or low energy. If you're procrastinating, doubting yourself, trying to control everything, or feeling stuck, these obstacles may be holding you back.

By understanding how you show up and how you are feeling (whether it's fear, perfectionism, or repeated stories in the form of limiting beliefs), you can change. With awareness and the right techniques, clarity and small steps, you gain confidence, self-belief and ultimately, greater impact.

KEY INSIGHTS

- **Your mind follows rules.**
  Learn them so they work for you, not against you.

- **Failure is feedback, not a final outcome.**

- **Perfectionism fuels procrastination and anxiety.**
  Progress matters more than perfection.

- **Managing your energy is just as important as managing your time.**

- **Your subconscious mind runs the show.**
  Be intentional about reprogramming it.

In the next chapter, we'll look at some personal client stories in detail and how they relate to transformation, consistency, values, and resilience.

CHAPTER 4:
Personal Stories of Transformation

"Your life does not get better by chance; it gets better by change."

— JIM ROHN

Transformation is not just a concept, it's a lived experience that shapes who we become. Every breakthrough I've had, every lesson I've learned, and every challenge I've overcome has fuelled my passion for helping others do the same.

The lessons I've learned in my journey, about mindset, resilience, and transformation, are the same ones that can help you create change in your own life.

Through my own experiences and the clients I've worked with, I've seen time and time again that it's what goes on in our mindset that is the key to unlocking new possibilities.

THE SEEDS OF CURIOSITY AND RESILIENCE

Growing up in Norfolk, England, with plenty of space to run wild, my childhood was shaped by two contrasting worlds. On the one side it was the predictable structure of my family's life: school, hard work, responsibility, and societal expectations. On the other side were nature, adventure, and the outdoors. I was born in Wymondham, Norfolk, and we were blessed with wide open spaces, where we could roam freely, which we did. Along with my brother, one year older than me, we frequently explored the lane outside our house. We were often drawn to one of the neighbours, a short distance down the lane, Peter and Pearl. Their unconventional, self-sufficient lifestyle fascinated me. They grew their own food, repurposed materials, and lived with a freedom that was the polar opposite of our more structured upbringing.

Their way of life sparked something in me, a deep curiosity about different ways of thinking and living. I questioned the traditional path laid out for me and always dreamt of adventure, challenges, and discovery.

As a lover of sports and the outdoors, I got an opportunity to try horse riding. I instantly fell in love with everything involved with riding, looking after horses, mucking out the stables, and grooming. Eventually my grandparents shared the cost and bought me a pony. I had to be resourceful, growing produce, cleaning cars and houses, mowing lawns to help pay the expenses. I competed in gymkhanas with my pony, Jimmy, before getting my horse, Pied

Piper. After that, I represented Norfolk in show jumping and one-day eventing.

At university, my adventurous spirit led me to become the first woman in my program to secure an overseas placement in my third year. It was the year out, working, that attracted me to this course in the beginning.

A year to gain life experiences and skills, rather than just studying in the classroom. I found myself in Ein Gedi, Israel, managing irrigation systems in the Negev Desert, hiking and connecting with varied and fascinating people. The experience reinforced what I had begun to suspect: stepping into the unknown builds confidence, broadens perspectives, opens the door to new opportunities, and sets the stage for transformation.

After graduating, I travelled extensively, spending six years exploring cultures, learning from people around the world, and questioning what truly makes people happy and successful. In Africa, I witnessed stark contrasts.

In Zaire, villagers with very little material wealth exuded joy, happily dancing and singing and welcoming foreigners to their villages, while in Zambia, highly paid expatriates seemed weighed down by stress and dissatisfaction. I spent a glorious week on the shores of Lake Malawi, spending time with the children, watching them laugh and play, creatively transforming old bottles, containers, and wood into scooters and other toys. These moments reinforced a powerful truth, success and fulfillment are not about wealth or status; they are cultivated from within.

FROM THE HUNZA VALLEY TO THE HAWAIIAN IRONMAN

One of the most defining moments of my travels happened in Pakistan's Hunza Valley. I attended a traditional wedding in an area where few tourists visited, let alone three English ladies! As tradition goes, the women were required to watch the festivities from the rooftops, while the men danced below. As we were visitors, we were welcome to join the celebration, as the ladies watched from outside, laughing and, I'm sure, wishing they could join in with us too. I realised how often we take our lives for granted. That moment deepened my commitment to making the most of my freedom and the choices we have, and embracing challenges and opportunities.

Years later, I put that mindset into action by competing in the Hawaii Ironman World Championships, one of the toughest endurance races in the world. Training required waking up at 4:30 a.m., balancing a demanding job, and pushing through physical and mental exhaustion. Some days, I wanted to quit, but my determination kept me going. Crossing that finish line in Hawaii solidified my belief in the power of mindset, resilience, and incremental progress.

That same belief drives the work I do today, helping others break through their barriers, change their thinking, rewire their minds, and achieve extraordinary results.

CLIENT STORIES OF TRANSFORMATION

JAMES:
Reconnecting with Purpose

James, a successful business owner, had steered his company through the challenges of the pandemic, but in the process, he had neglected himself. When we first spoke, he said, *"I feel flat. I've lost my spark."* He wasn't sleeping well, had stopped exercising, and couldn't remember the last time he did something just for fun. Through small, intentional changes such as morning rituals, exercise, and reintroducing hobbies that brought him joy, James began to feel like himself again. Within weeks, his motivation returned, his energy lifted, and both his relationships and business started to flourish.

TINA:
Choosing Freedom

Tina came to me seeking help as she felt trapped in a toxic relationship and a soul-crushing job. Together, we created a plan and a vision for her future. Next we cleared the limiting beliefs holding her back. With newfound courage, she left her job, pursued her passion for interior design, and spent a year travelling solo in a campervan. Tina's journey underscores the power of aligning with one's values, being courageous, and embracing challenges and the unfamiliar. Fast forward to today, and she is now focusing on helping people step into their full potential, leaning on her personal journey of transformation.

FINAL THOUGHTS

Every transformation begins with a single decision, the decision to change. To step beyond your comfort zone, be brave enough to dig deep and get to know yourself at a deeper level. Ask some tough questions, set a new direction for your future, and commit to your new path. Whether it's a shift in thinking, stepping up to take action, or a new perspective on your direction, this sets in motion the potential to profound transformation.

Your journey is uniquely yours, but the principles remain the same. By embracing curiosity, working from the inside out, and taking intentional action, leads to a new level of fulfilment and success.

KEY INSIGHTS

- **Transformation begins within.**
  Change starts with self-awareness and a willingness to act.

- **Small steps create big results.**
  Consistent, intentional actions compound into significant progress.

- **Your mindset shapes your reality.**
  Aligning thoughts and actions with your values fuels growth and fulfilment.

- **Resilience is built over time.**
  Facing challenges head-on strengthens your capacity to adapt and thrive.

In the next chapter we'll explore the REWIRE Model, a powerful framework to help you retrain your brain, shift your thinking, and cultivate a high-performance mindset for personal and professional excellence.

CHAPTER 5:
The REWIRE Model For High-Performance

"There's a future you out there that already has a greater mind. And you meet that person by taking the time to be a creator in your life."

— DR. JOE DISPENZA

WHY REWIRE?

Now that we've explored the power of mindset and uncovered the hidden barriers that hold you back, it's time to delve deeper. It's taking intentional action that leads to real and lasting transformation.

This is where the REWIRE Model comes in. One that provides a structured approach to help you understand yourself, train, tame and rewire your brain to elevate your performance, and create meaningful and more excellent results.

Driving this process is neuroplasticity. Perhaps one of the most fascinating recent discoveries, the brain has an ability to form new neural connections and reshape itself based on your thoughts, habits, and actions.

WHAT DOES IT MEAN TO REWIRE YOUR BRAIN?

Every thought you think strengthens a neural pathway. The more you repeat a thought, belief, or action, the stronger it becomes, like carving a deeper groove into a well-worn path. Over time, these reinforced patterns become automatic, shaping your mindset, behaviours and results. This is what is called self-directed neuroplasticity. Your thoughts generate neural activity, and your brain has the ability to rewire itself based on what you consistently focus on. When you intentionally work on training your brain to prioritise thoughts and beliefs that empower you rather than limit you, are on the way to creating a new future.

Neuroscientist Dr. Michael Merzenich explains:

*"Your brain… is a work in progress.
It continuously revises and remodels itself as a
function of how we use it."*

The exciting part? You have the power to direct this process and intentionally create the life you want. Whether it's overcoming self-doubt, building confidence or breaking free from old patterns, rewiring your brain puts you in control of your future and your growth.

HARNESSING ENERGY

At the heart and around the REWIRE Model is energy. Everything in the universe, including our thoughts, emotions and actions, is made up of energy.

Albert Einstein famously said:

"Everything is energy."

Quantum physics provides compelling evidence for the power of energy and intention. In the well-known double-slit experiment, scientists discovered that the simple act of observation altered the behaviour of particles, showing that consciousness and intention influence physical matter. This supports a key principle of the REWIRE Model: directing your energy with intention shapes your outcomes.

Energy fuels every aspect of our lives. How we think, how we perform, and how we feel.

Your mental, emotional, and physical energy influences your decisions, performance, and the results you create. When your energy is aligned, you feel clear, motivated and driven. When it is scattered or drained, everything feels harder. Intentionally managing your energy boosts your focus, positivity, empowerment, and ability to act strategically toward your goals.

THE REWIRE MODEL EXPLAINED

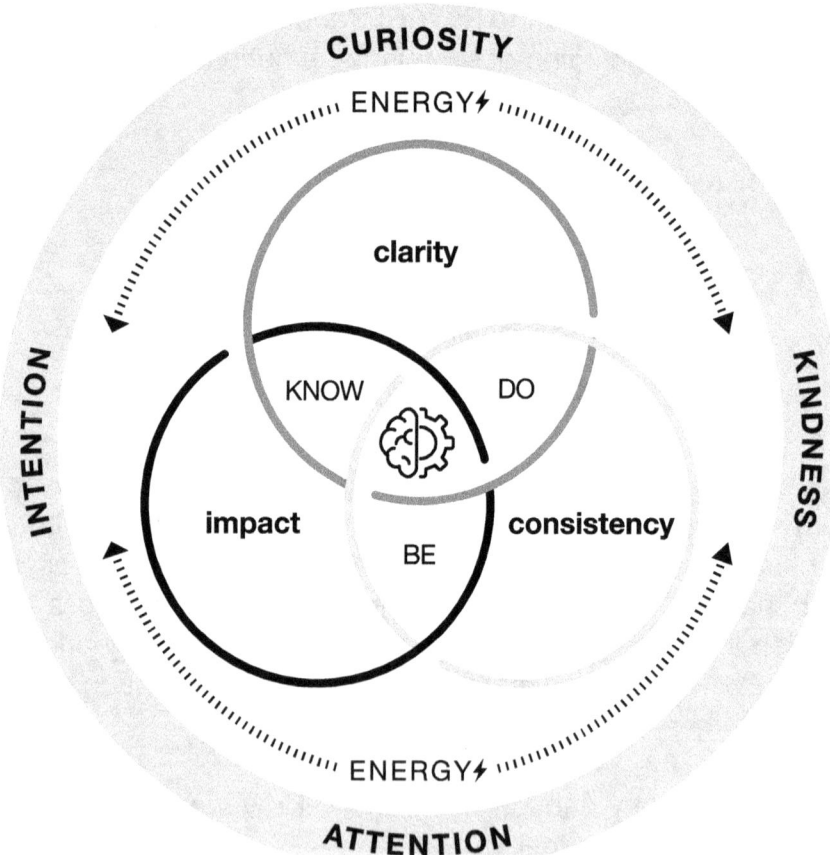

The Outer Circle

Surrounding the core of the REWIRE Model is an outer circle, with four essential elements that shape how you engage with the world: curiosity, kindness, intention, and attention. These four energies act as guiding forces, influencing and elevating your ability to create lasting change. Though intangible, they serve as powerful lenses through which you perceive and navigate life.

Curiosity: The Spark That Ignites Growth

Curiosity fuels learning, creativity, and growth. When you are curious, you are in the energy of possibility and potential, a higher energy state. When our energy is high, we are more motivated and productive.

A Harvard study found that reflecting on moments of curiosity throughout the day increased energy levels by 20%. Additionally, research by neuroscientist Jaak Panksepp reveals that curiosity and play are two core emotions present in all mammals, reinforcing that curiosity is essential for a healthy, engaged brain.

Curiosity also plays a key role in neuroplasticity, causing the brain to form new neural connections. When you explore new ideas, ask questions, and challenge assumptions, you activate and strengthen neural pathways, rewiring the brain. Moreover, it enhances cognitive flexibility, deepens learning, and increases adaptability.

By fostering a mindset of curiosity, you don't just expand your thinking, you actively reshape your brain, creating the conditions for new growth and development.

Kindness: The Key to Growth and Confidence

Kindness is the other half of the lens to curiosity. It is a powerful yet often overlooked element of growth. Kindness starts with how you treat yourself. When you replace self-criticism with self-compassion, you elevate your state and create space to learn, adapt, and improve. New possibilities show up, and growth becomes possible. Being unkind to yourself minimises your confidence and stops you from flourishing.

One of the most prevalent patterns I see in high achievers is their ability to speak harshly to themselves and minimise their personal power.

On a physiological level, kindness boosts serotonin and dopamine, the neurotransmitters responsible for feelings of satisfaction and well-being. This activates the brain's pleasure and reward centres, reinforcing positive behaviours and supporting identity-level growth. Kindness also strengthens your connection with others, fosters deeper relationships and a greater sense of belonging.

Kindness is an intangible asset, difficult to measure yet deeply impactful. When combined with curiosity, you have two high-energy forces that take you to an expansive place of possibility.

Dr. Daniel Amen, from the Brain Clinic, who has extensively researched the brain and what harms it, emphasises that negative thinking disrupts healthy brain function, increasing stress and anxiety. When you are unkind to yourself, your inner dialogue often turns negative, reinforcing limiting beliefs, depleting mental energy, and diminishing well-being. By practicing kindness towards yourself, you interrupt this cycle, creating a healthier brain environment and fostering a more positive, growth-oriented mindset.

Attention: The Currency of Life and High Performance

Attention is your most valuable mental resource. It is the energy of the mind. It directs your energy, shapes your focus, and determines your reality.

Dr. Joe Dispenza explains:

"Life is about the management of energy. Where you place your attention is where you place your energy."

Mastering attention is a key habit to cultivate, as it enhances self-awareness. When you are self-aware, you can more easily see your blind spots, reveal and change hidden habits, limiting beliefs, and strengthen neural pathways.

A great example of how focused attention enhances learning comes from research on London taxi drivers. Neuroscientists found that drivers have a larger hippocampus, the area of the brain linked to spatial memory, due to the intense mental training needed for navigation.

To earn their qualification, known as *The Knowledge*, they must memorise thousands of streets and landmarks, as well as the most efficient routes between any two points in the city.

This rigorous practice physically reshapes their brains, reinforcing the connection between attention and neuroplasticity.

Just as their brains adapt through deliberate training, you too can strengthen your mind and lock in new behaviours by consistently and intentionally focusing your attention on what you want to learn or change.

By mastering your attention, you can:

- Recognise and replace limiting beliefs and unhelpful habits.
- Increase emotional awareness.
- Ensure your self-talk is consistently positive.
- Maintain focus and reduce distractions, such as bright, shiny objects.
- Improve decision-making and respond thoughtfully instead of reacting impulsively.

You must treat your attention like money. Invest it wisely in what truly matters, and it will take care of you. Greater clarity, confidence, performance, and results.

Intention: The Power of Directed Energy

*"Excellence is never an accident.
It is always the result of high intention,
sincere effort, and intelligent execution."*

— ARISTOTLE

When you set an intention, you steer the energy of your mind towards your desired outcome. Just as attention powerfully directs where your energy flows, intention purposefully focuses that energy on a specific destination. Without clear intentions, your actions are often driven by habits and unconscious patterns rather than conscious choice. With intention, you powerfully steer the direction of your life.

The word 'intention' comes from the Latin intendere, meaning 'to stretch toward.' When you set an intention, you are stretching your focus and energy into your future, programming your mind to prioritise what matters.

When you set an intention, the Reticular Activating System (RAS), a part of your brain that filters incoming information based on what it deems important, comes into play. Like a beam of light, it highlights what you are focusing on, helping you attune to relevant opportunities, raising their importance, making it easier to notice and act on them. Conversely, when you aren't intentional, your RAS filters out new possibilities and highlights what it already knows: your old programs and beliefs. The power of intention and the RAS is often experienced in daily life. Have you ever thought about someone and then they suddenly call? Or made a firm decision, only to have the right resources or people appear at the perfect time? That's your RAS at work, filtering the vast amount of information around you to align with your focus.

By setting and reinforcing clear intentions, you direct your energy with purpose, making meaningful progress towards your goals.

When paired with visualisation and positive feelings, intentions become even more powerful, as the brain processes vivid mental images as though they were real. Feelings are the language of the body, while thoughts are the language of the mind. Combined, they strengthen neural pathways, increase connection, and help build self-belief in your ability to achieve them.

Cultivating curiosity, kindness, attention, and intention sets the foundation for rewiring your brain, creating a high-performance mindset, and achieving your highest potential.

THE KEY COMPONENTS OF THE REWIRE MODEL

The REWIRE Model has three key circles and three components that connect. All work independently and synergistically.

1. Clarity: Knowing Yourself and Your Path Forward

Clarity is the beginning of transformation. If you don't know what you want, it's impossible to achieve it. But clarity isn't just about goals and knowing what you want; it's also about deeply understanding yourself.

Clarity means:

- **Knowing yourself from the inside out.**
  Understanding your values, strengths, beliefs, and what truly drives you. Becoming aware of your limiting beliefs and old patterns, and transforming them.

- **Creating a vision and a clear path forward.**
  Getting clear on your goals, priorities, and what actions are required.

- **Removing distractions.**
  Eliminating what steals your focus and keeps you from moving forward.

- **Understanding energy.**
  Knowing what increases your energy and what drains it.

Without self-awareness, external goals can feel misaligned or unfulfilling. But when you combine self-knowledge with a clear direction, you gain the confidence, energy, and focus to move forward with purpose.

Combining self-knowledge with a clear direction boosts your confidence, energy, and focus, allowing you to move forward purposefully.

The deeper you get to know yourself, from the inside out, the greater your alignment and chances of success. With a clear vision and goals, you build confidence, energy and motivation to move forward purposefully.

When Sulaiman contacted me, he was already on the path of personal development and had a high level of awareness, working with top coaches and completing several of Tony Robbins' programs. Yet, despite his achievements, he knew he wasn't operating at his full potential. One of his biggest challenges was building a consistent morning routine. Every few weeks, he would keep tripping himself up, unable to make it stick, for one reason or another, such as being unwell or having a late-night function. He felt he was unknowingly sabotaging his success, yet couldn't pinpoint why.

Through our work together, I helped him uncover a deeply ingrained childhood belief that was still at play. As a youngster, he used to frequently sleep in, and his father told him he would never be a morning person.

This story created an unconscious belief, an invisible yet powerful barrier to his success, shaping his identity without him realising it, and blocking his potential. Once he recognised it for what it was, just an outdated belief, he transformed the energy from a limiting belief to an empowering belief. He chose to believe that he was the type of person who could easily fall in love with getting up early. Ultimately, he changed his story, rewired his brain, and shifted the trajectory of his life.

From that moment, he fully committed to his morning routine, which became the linchpin of his day. He was successful for two weeks, four weeks, and then three months, consistently getting up on time.

With this newfound structure, despite a full-time job, he has more energy and focus to advance his startup company and lifelong vision: tackling the global loneliness epidemic by developing an innovative solution, building an app to help people connect.

Four years later, we continue working together, and I'm honoured to be part of his company, Konnect, with a role as the high-performance mindset coach. My mission: to help everyone perform at their peak while achieving lasting fulfilment. Sulaiman's story is a testament to how discovering and shifting the power of our unconscious patterns and rewiring the brain can transform results.

Even the most accomplished individuals have blind spots, and sometimes, a single shift in perspective is all it takes to unlock the next level of success.

2. Consistency: The Power of Daily Action

The secret to rewiring your brain and achieving success is consistent, repeated actions. Small daily actions compound over time, reinforcing new beliefs, thought patterns, and behaviours until they become second nature. Working on your mental and emotional state is just as important as creating physical habits of action.

Repeatedly choosing empowering thoughts and reframing limiting beliefs helps you reinforce a new narrative. The more you do this, the more your brain rewires itself to support it.

Years ago, NASA did an upside-down goggles experiment to simulate and determine the impact of stress on their bodies in preparation for going to space. Astronauts wore vision-flipping goggles 24/7, and after 26 to 30 consecutive days, their brains rewired themselves to see the world normally again. Taking this a step further, they interrupted the process by allowing certain participants to take their goggles off for short durations.

The findings? When the experiment was interrupted before reaching that threshold, the rewiring process was interrupted, and they had to restart from the beginning.

The lesson? Consistency isn't just important, it's non-negotiable for rewiring the brain and creating real, lasting change. Furthermore, depending on what you want to change, it may take far longer than 30 days.

3. Impact: The Ripple Effect of Your Actions

Impact is the result of clarity, consistency, and aligned action. However, it's not just about what you accomplish, it's about the effect you have on others.

The more aligned and intentional you are, the greater the ripple effect you create in your work, relationships, and life.

Sulaiman didn't just redefine his vision, he inspired and continually inspires the team to innovate and execute at a high level, impacting their potential for growth, belief, and mindset positively.

When you commit to your personal growth, your influence and impact can be profound.

4. Know Yourself: Become Self-Aware

Self-awareness is the foundation of change and growth. To rewire your brain and elevate your performance, you must first understand:

- What thoughts and habits are holding you back?
- What patterns have shaped your current reality?
- What limiting beliefs need to be released and changed to align with your goals?
- What are your strengths, and how can you leverage them?
- Where are your weaknesses, and how can you improve them or adapt?
- What self-sabotaging patterns keep repeating in your life?
- What energises you, and what drains you?

By choosing to work on yourself, knowing and becoming aware of what makes you tick, you build the power to shift and change what isn't serving you.

5. Do: Turning Knowledge into Action

Knowing isn't enough. You must take action, even when it's uncomfortable. Action is the antidote to doubt, and the catalyst of change. Moreover, neuroplasticity requires repetition and consistent, intentional action.

6. Be: Be Your Best!

The final piece of the REWIRE model is identity: who you choose to be. Success and fulfillment aren't just about external achievements. They're about doing the things you say you will do and ensuring your thoughts, actions, and behaviours are aligned with your values and purpose. This is how to shape your identity and become a better version of yourself.

And here's the key: The more you step into your best self, the greater your impact. When you embody confidence, resilience, and authenticity, you don't just elevate your own life, you inspire and influence those around you. The energy you bring to the world ripples outward, shaping your relationships, work, and the legacy you leave behind.

Your greatest impact begins with the decision to become the person who already embodies the success, mindset, and habits you seek. When you focus on being, the doing and results naturally follow.

Identity — Your Core Energy

If you take a closer look at the heart of the REWIRE Model, you will find the central force shaping your life: your identity, your core energy. It is not always obvious, but it influences everything.

Who you are at your core, your beliefs, mindset, and values, radiates outward, shaping your habits, decisions, and impact.

Think of it like the engine of a high-performance sports car. Just as an engine determines a car's power, speed, and efficiency, your core energy fuels how you show up in life. When your energy is aligned, when your thoughts, beliefs, and actions reflect your true identity, you move through life with clarity, purpose, and impact.

But just like an engine, your identity requires regular tuning. Without self-awareness and alignment between your conscious and subconscious mind, you risk drifting into disconnection. When your identity is out of sync with your actions, you create resistance in your energy. You are likely to feel frustration, overwhelm, resignation, or some other unhelpful state, which drains the very energy you need to succeed.

As philosopher and author Alain de Botton warns:

"There is real danger of a disconnect between what is on your business card and who you are deep inside."

Take Carol, for example. She knew what she wanted and was taking action, yet the results were not materialising. When we uncovered and cleared her limiting belief, it was like a floodgate opening. Her energy shifted, and her self-belief grew, unlocking new possibilities and positively impacting her internal and external world. With this transformation at the level of identity, and her new level of self-belief, she achieved her goal, successfully listing and selling million-dollar properties.

When you work on ensuring both parts of your mind are aligned: your thoughts, goals, actions, values, and habits, your core energy radiates out, your self-belief grows, positively influencing and impacting the external world.

The Power of Rewiring Your Brain

The REWIRE Model is here to help you know yourself, gain clarity, and take consistent action in the direction of your future. Moreover, to help you become the best version of yourself. Know, do, and be, to build self-belief and create great and excellent performances.

KEY INSIGHTS

✓ **Neuroplasticity** means your brain can change, grow, and adapt at any stage of life.

✓ **Your energy shapes your thoughts, emotions, and actions.**
It's the driving force behind change and success.

✓ **Awareness is the first step to transformation;** building unshakeable self-belief is key.

✓ **Success isn't just about doing;** it's about who you choose to be.

ACTION STEPS

- **Assess where you are now.**
Are you clear on what you want and why? Do you truly know yourself? Review your High-Performance Mindset Self-Assessment Questionnaire.

- **Focus on becoming more aware.**
Imagine you are an observer, curiously looking at yourself and how you operate. Observe yourself daily. Are you focused? Do you take intentional action? What happens when you have a setback?

- **Track your energy.**
Where is your attention? Is it directed towards what you want or away from what you don't want? When do you feel energised, and when do you feel drained?

These small but deliberate shifts will lay the foundation for rewiring your brain and developing a high-performance mindset that drives long-term success.

CHAPTER 6:
Building Clarity — Inside Out Work

"We cannot become what we need to be by remaining what we are."

— OPRAH WINFREY

In this chapter, we are going to focus on two areas: A) Knowing what you want and B) Knowing yourself from the inside out.

CHOOSING A DESTINATION

One of the first exercises I guide my clients through is creating a compelling vision for their lives. We usually focus on a 12-month vision. This provides a clear destination, much like planning a road trip from Brisbane to Sydney. While there may be various routes to get there and stops along the way, having a destination to head towards keeps you focused. It gives your brain direction. When we make our vision stronger and more compelling than what we currently have, it starts to show up in the outer world. Our brains are constantly making new connections as we experience life, learn new ideas, patterns, and skills. This first step helps us retrain our brains to new levels of what's possible.

Imagine yourself standing 12 months into the future, reflecting on a year filled with success, great memories, and growth. Connect with the emotions you will feel, such as pride, joy, and calm. Consider key areas of your life: health, wealth, career, relationships, contribution, and lifestyle. Include moments of fun, connection, and personal and professional achievements. Aim for a minimum of 3-5 key goals, and remember — version one is better than version none!

Start with: *"I am so grateful for the amazing year I've had..."* Then outline what you have achieved, gained, or become. Here are a few examples:

- *"I am so grateful for sticking to my exercise goals. I completed a half-marathon in under one hour fifty and loved the freedom and strength I gained from my training."*

- *"I am so grateful I hired a new staff member to handle administration and finances. She's done an amazing job, giving me back four hours a week to focus on growing the business."*

- *"I'm so grateful we installed new software that reduced inefficiencies by 20% and increased our revenue by 25%."*

- *"I am so grateful for the weekends away with my family each month. We laughed, reconnected, and made lasting memories."*

> To help you craft your own vision, download a template from the **REWIRE Resources Portal**.

GOALS

Goals give us purpose and meaning and help us grow and achieve. Research has found that people who score high on life purpose live longer, healthier, and more fulfilling lives. (Naomi Simson, *'Live What You Love'*)

Now, it's time to identify 3-5 goals that make up your vision. If you consistently reach your goals, choose five. If you tend to get overwhelmed, focus on no more than three key priorities that matter most to you.

Renowned psychologist Edwin Locke emphasises that specific, challenging goals lead to higher performance. His research suggests that people who clearly define their goals and set measurable, time-bound objectives are more likely to stay motivated and take effective action.

Locke's five principles align closely with my six-step CLEARer Goals Method. This process ensures that you are clear, connected, and committed to pursuing your goal.

> You can download a copy of the CLEARer Goals template in the **REWIRE Resources Portal**.

CLEARER GOALS

> *"The regrets of not having walked down those roads will often outweigh the fears you inhabited of what worse could come along the journey."*
>
> — RUMI

First, physically write out your goal. Writing down your goals strengthens neural pathways, improving both retention and focus.

As Dr. Judy Willis emphasises:

> *"The practice of writing can enhance the brain's intake, processing, retaining, and retrieving of information. It promotes the brain's attentive focus, boosts long-term memory, illuminates patterns."*

This is the format I suggest:

---

*"It is now October 30th, 2025,
and I am looking at my bank statement,
which shows $250,000 — a doubling of my
income. I feel thrilled and proud."*

Reading your goal aloud daily strengthens your connection to it and makes it more familiar. This alignment strengthens motivation and increases your chances of high performance and success.

Now let's unpack the CLEARer methodology

STEP 1: C = CONCISE

Clearly define your goal in one or two sentences, adding measurable outcomes (e.g., double fitness levels, increase income by 50%, complete a half-marathon in under two hours). Write the goal in the present tense, with a deadline.

STEP 2: L = LOOK

Imagine what your life looks like from the place of goal achievement. Picture yourself at that moment, looking through your own eyes. Make this image as vivid, bright, and detailed as possible. Engage all your senses — what you see, hear, taste, smell, and most importantly, feel. Regular mental rehearsal strengthens this image in your mind, helping to embed it into your neurology and build belief.

As Neville Goddard teaches:

"Assume the feeling of the wish fulfilled."

Be in the experience of achieving it, rather than being on the way.

STEP 3: E = ENERGISE

Your goal should genuinely excite and energise you. Doubt or lack of enthusiasm may show that you have limiting beliefs or that your goal doesn't match your true desires.

Are you pursuing this goal for yourself or someone else? Refine your goal until it feels fully aligned and sparks genuine excitement. Deci and Ryan's Self-Determination Theory highlights that intrinsic motivation leads to enhanced performance, sustained effort, and a greater ability to cope with challenges.

STEP 4: A = ACTION

Identify the specific actions required to achieve your goal. Equally important is recognising what you might need to sacrifice. Every choice has a cost and benefit, and success often requires letting go of certain comforts or habits. Carefully consider what you're willing to sacrifice to make your goal a reality. Weigh these benefits against the costs of inaction. What would it mean to you if you failed to achieve this goal? Without this awareness, setbacks may feel overwhelming and cause you to hesitate, or even quit. For example:

- If you enjoy sleeping in, you might need to get up earlier to exercise.
- If you want to study for an MBA, you may need to reduce your Netflix time or family time to work on it.
- If you want to improve your finances, you may need to create a stricter budget.

By taking the necessary actions, you build self-belief and prove to yourself that you are capable of achieving what you set out to do. A vital point.

STEP 5: R = REVIEW

Action creates results, and results require review. Carefully review your plan so far. Are you fully prepared to commit to your goal? Do you believe you can maintain consistency? What about the sacrifices? Are you willing to do what it takes? If doubts arise, identify potential obstacles and address them proactively.

---

*"The major reason for setting goals
is to compel you to become the person
it takes to achieve them."*

— JIM ROHN

STEP 6: er = EMOTIONAL REASON

Write down as many reasons as possible for why you want this goal. After you've done that, identify one of those reasons as the key reason why you want this goal. Keep searching until you uncover a core emotion like freedom, pride, or joy. This emotional connection fuels motivation and should inspire you to keep going.

Example from a former client:

- **Goal:**
  Pursue an MBA

- **Question:**
  What will completing an MBA give you that is even more important?

- **Answer:**
  Respect in my business and more skills

- **Question:**
  What will having respect in your business and more skills give you that is even more important?

- **Answer:**
  More clients through greater trust and credibility

- **Question:**
  And what will this give you?

- **Answer:**
  It will give me more income and financial abundance.

- **Question:**
  What will having financial abundance give you?

- **Answer:**
  It will give me choices and freedom. I will create a successful business that allows me to set my own hours and follow my passions.

- **Core Emotional Driver:**
  Freedom — the ability to choose when and how to work.

Remember:

"People don't buy what you do; they buy why you do it."

— SIMON SINEK

CREATING A PLAN

Just like building a house requires a detailed architectural blueprint, achieving your life goals demands a well-structured plan. A clear roadmap keeps you aligned with your vision and prevents you from drifting aimlessly.

For each goal, consider whether it consists of smaller goals or projects. It can be helpful to break a goal into smaller pieces, as each one might have varied and many steps. For example, doubling your business may consist of four goals, or projects. For example, you may have to focus on hiring staff, improving systems, a new marketing strategy, and social media presence. Breaking the big goal into smaller goals, or projects, helps prevent overwhelm. Next, list the critical steps for each goal in five or six bullet points. Writing these steps down provides direction and serves as a reference point when setbacks arise or uncertainty creeps in.

Roy Baumeister, a leading social psychologist, found that committing to a specific plan frees up cognitive resources.

When you know the steps ahead, your brain has more capacity to focus on execution rather than constantly questioning the next move. Studies also show that people who plan experience lower stress levels, greater job satisfaction, and improved problem-solving skills.

Additionally, writing down goals and creating a structured plan helps avoid cognitive overload, where your brain fixates on uncompleted tasks, leading to anxiety and mental fatigue.

Specific, written plans are what help rewire the brain and drive real change.

Take a leaf from Stephen Covey's *The 7 Habits of Highly Effective People*, and embrace Habit 3: *"Put First Things First."* Focus on what truly matters and consistently act on high-priority tasks, regardless of your mood or distractions.

Ask Yourself:

- "What goal(s) am I working towards?"
- "Is this merely interesting, or is it important?"
- "Is this action moving me closer to my goals?"
- "Are my actions aligned with my core values?"

THE POWER OF THOUGHTS

Clarity increases by understanding the power of our thoughts and the language we use daily. Indeed, mastering our thoughts, especially those that don't serve us, is a key ingredient of a high-performance mindset. And that is a big task, as we have between 50,000 and 70,000 thoughts per day. Our inner dialogue never stops. The stories we tell ourselves and the messages we take in become the lens through which we view our lives. Our narrative, whether helpful or harmful, shapes our lives, results and reality.

Daniel Kahneman reminds us that these messages don't even need to be true:

> *"A message, unless it is immediately rejected as a lie, will have the same effect on the associative system regardless of its reliability. Whether the story is true or believable matters little, if at all."*

Imagine your mind as a fishing net trawling through the sea. It collects all sorts of debris: old fishing lines, plastic bags, and even large fish. If you don't pay attention to what gets caught, your net can become clogged with waste, just like negative and toxic thoughts can accumulate in your mind. Over time, if left unchecked, these repeated thoughts become ingrained habits, influencing how you think, feel, and act.

Furthermore, your brain actively seeks to bring into reality what it believes.

As Henry Ford famously said:

"Whether you think you can or think you can't, you're right."

Paying attention to your thoughts can change the course of your life. Our brains are wired to seek patterns, much like a net attracting fish. By consciously choosing empowering thoughts, you can shift your internal environment and radically improve your life.

THOUGHTS BECOME INGRAINED HABITS

Many of our thoughts run on autopilot, because they have become habits. Consequently, we aren't aware of what we are saying most of the time, and don't realise the power of thoughts to shape our behaviours and decisions, and the trajectory of our lives. A striking example of this comes from a well-known study by social psychologist John Bargh in 1996. Participants were given single-word flashcards and asked to construct sentences. Unbeknownst to them, some groups were given words related to ageing, such as wrinkle, forgetful, grey, walking stick, and arthritis.

After completing the task, participants walked down a hallway to sign out while being timed. The results were fascinating: those who had been exposed to age-related words walked more slowly than those who had not.

This phenomenon, known as the "Florida Effect," suggests that our environment and the words we internalise can subconsciously shape our behaviour. Though some debate remains about the experiment's interpretation, modern research supports the idea that repeated exposure to certain words and ideas physically rewires the brain; an essential concept in neuroplasticity.

When you think a thought, your brain releases chemicals that flood your body, reinforcing the emotional state that aligns with that thought. Thinking about a past failure can trigger stress and self-doubt, while thinking about a past success can generate confidence and motivation.

MY HAWAII STORY

Our thoughts are truly powerful, and with careful management, you can use them to change the direction of your life and achieve different results. I have experienced this phenomenon firsthand many times. However, one of my most memorable experiences with the power of words came during the Hawaii Ironman in Kona, the ultimate test of endurance for long-distance triathletes.

On race day, I recall standing at the starting line, feeling nervous and unsure of my ability to complete this gruelling race. I wasn't sure I'd even make it to the start line. A few days after arriving in Hawaii, I became sick with a debilitating cough that prevented me from any training before the race. But one of my strongest personal philosophies, deeply embedded in my identity, is: *"Never, ever, ever quit on yourself."*

As the whistle blew, and the race began, we all entered the water together. It was like a human washing machine, with legs and arms thrashing in the water as people swam over each other to get ahead. Already struggling, I swallowed some water, and then my goggles got kicked off. Doubts and fatigue started to creep in.

As I somewhat exhaustedly exited the water and made it to the bike transition, just a few hundred metres into the bike leg, my spare water bottle cage, supposedly attached securely to my seat post, fell off. Ironically, right in front of my coach, who sensing my hesitancy, told me to keep going. Doubts crept in because there are two major challenges in this race. The intense heat and the extreme crosswinds, both leading to dehydration, which can destroy one's chances of finishing the race.

I could feel the intense heat, a searing 38°C, and the crosswinds were brutal. Now, negative thoughts were creeping in: *"Can I really do this?" "Maybe it's okay to pull out. I didn't even know if I would be able to race anyway."*

At that moment, feeling lonely, vulnerable and close to defeat, I am not sure what changed, but it was like an inner power arose from deep within. A voice that reminded me we are stronger than we think we are, and my deep philosophy of never, ever, ever quit on yourself, came to my mind.

I realised something: my thoughts were sabotaging me, and if I didn't change them, these dream stealers would destroy my dreams.

I made a conscious decision to mentally reset and 'STOP' this old story. I changed my internal dialogue.

Instead of battling the wind, I knew I had to 'befriend the enemy.' I told myself, *"The wind is my friend."*

I repeated this mantra over and over, and, if by magic, I felt my energy shift. Within moments, the wind felt less overpowering. I felt lighter and more hopeful, regaining momentum. The negative thoughts melted away, and I kept focusing on my new mantra.

When we see things differently, the things around us shift. Suddenly, I experienced things that helped lift my spirits. A cyclist passed me and gave me words of encouragement. Next, the wind felt like it stopped for a few minutes. Approaching the turnaround, I saw my friend, Minnie, on her way back, and I realised I wasn't far behind. As this elevated my spirits, I saw a cyclist with one leg cycling towards the turnaround. If he could do this, then so could I.

I pedalled on and made it to the transition, before the last piece, a 42.2-kilometre run. I changed my mantra to, *"Every step is a step nearer."*

Thirteen hours after starting, I finally crossed the finish line, two and a quarter hours slower than my time at Forster, the Australian Ironman Championships, but a finisher, nonetheless. I truly believe, to this day, changing my thoughts in that moment changed the race in my favour.

THE SCIENCE OF THOUGHT AND ENERGY

Our words and thoughts have the power to elevate or deflate us, and shape our physical and emotional state. Research shows that just by thinking about someone you love can cause structural changes in the brain's caudate nucleus, an area associated with learning and reward.

Conversely, dwelling on stress or negativity strengthens neural pathways associated with anxiety and worry. Studies suggest that chronic stress and negative thought patterns can contribute to cognitive decline, even increasing the risk of Alzheimer's.

Your thoughts are waves of energy that shape your brain's structure and chemistry, reinforcing the principles of neuroplasticity. Every thought you have influences your body, emotions, and ultimately, the life you create. Remember this. And make it a lifelong habit to observe and master your mind.

A Powerful Technique to Release Negative Thoughts: The Positive Self-Talk Optimiser

To change your thoughts, you must first become aware of them. Next, you must release the old and replace it with a new and empowering thought. Here is a simple yet powerful tool I teach my clients to help rewire their inner dialogue and release negative thoughts.

THE POSITIVE SELF-TALK OPTIMISER

OBSERVE

The first step is awareness. Imagine yourself as a detective, curiously eavesdropping on your own inner dialogue. Simply observe and notice what you are telling yourself. Embrace a mindset of curiosity and kindness.

RELEASE

Once you identify a negative thought, you must release it, and here, you can be as creative as you like. Use a visualisation technique that works for you:

Imagine the thought floating away like a balloon.

See it evaporate like steam.

Watch it disappear as you say *"Delete, delete."*

By acknowledging it first, then releasing it, you weaken its grip. Most people unknowingly fuel their negative thoughts by engaging with them, giving them more power and turning them into mental monsters.

REPLACE

Now, you must replace the old thought with a new one. Never leave an empty space, because everything is energy. Always fill the space and replace the old thought with something empowering.

For example, if your persistent thought is:
"I always get things wrong."

Change it to:
"Every day, I am stepping into the energy of success and easily getting better at what I do."

This simple shift retrains your brain to focus on possibilities rather than limitations.
Now that you understand the power of your thoughts and have a tool to help release negative patterns, it's time to dive deeper and explore your core values.

> Visit the **REWIRE Resources Portal** to download a copy of this technique.

KNOW WHAT IS IMPORTANT — VALUES

*"Values are like fingerprints.
Nobody's are the same, but you leave 'em all over everything you do."*

— ELVIS PRESLEY

Creating a high-performance mindset means gaining clarity about who you are, what matters most, and how you choose to show up in the world. Your values are the foundation of that clarity. They shape your decisions, guide your actions, and ultimately define your success.

When your values align with your goals, you create a powerful internal drive that makes it easier to stay focused and committed. You no longer chase things out of obligation or distraction. Instead, you move forward with purpose, making decisions that are aligned, intentional, and sustainable. This alignment strengthens your ability to stay consistent, which is the key to long-term success.

The Power of Values in Action

To illustrate the power of values, let me share the story of Jodie, a highly successful business owner dedicated to personal growth. Despite her achievements, she felt she was letting herself down by struggling to make exercise a consistent habit.

When we explored her values, she realised that family was, and had always been, her highest priority. However, through deeper reflection, she had a breakthrough; she saw that by prioritising morning exercise, she wasn't taking away from her family time, but actually enhancing it.

By committing to early workouts, she felt more in control of her day and developed greater discipline in caring for herself. As a result, she arrived at work energised, made better decisions, and felt more productive. When she returned home, she was fully present with her children and spouse, bringing more joy and connection to her family life. The impact? Increased fitness, renewed energy, improved focus, stronger relationships, and even greater success in her business.

Her transformation didn't come from willpower alone; it came from knowing herself and what was important; aligning her habits with her values. When you are clear on your values, what's important, consistency becomes easier, because what you are doing isn't just another task, it's a reflection of who you are.

DISCOVERING YOUR CORE VALUES

Your values are deeply personal, and they serve as your inner compass. To uncover your values, take a moment to reflect on your life:

- What truly matters to you?
- When do you feel most fulfilled, proud, or at peace?
- What principles guide your decisions and behaviours?
- What do you always make time for, no matter how busy life gets?

Values aren't just words; they create an emotional response. When you identify a core value, you *feel* it — it resonates deeply rather than just sounding good on paper. Moreover, when you can explain it to yourself deeply, you strengthen the connection which aids decision making and behaviours.

Examples of Core Values

Here are some common values to help guide your reflection. Choose the ones that resonate with you and consider what they mean in your life.

Achievement	Adventure	Authenticity	Balance
Challenge	Commitment	Compassion	Connection
Creativity	Discipline	Empowerment	Excellence
Family	Freedom	Growth	Health
Honesty	Impact	Independence	Integrity
Joy	Leadership	Learning	Love
Passion	Perseverance	Purpose	Resilience
Security	Self-Discipline	Service	Success
Trust	Vitality	Wealth	Wisdom

As you review this list, write down any additional values that come to mind. Then, refine your list to six to nine values that feel most essential to you.

ASPIRATIONAL VALUES

You may also have *aspirational values,* qualities you wish to cultivate more deeply, such as consistency, patience, or courage. Acknowledge these too, and look for ways to integrate them into your daily life. These could be values that have a deep meaning to you and you've been improving them for many years, and you want to grow in them even more.

They are often deeply rooted in childhood experiences where we had negative experiences that we want to move away from: for example, you may have experienced bullying in your childhood, and at the time you didn't know how to stand up to the bullies. So one of your aspirational values in this case might be courage. Likewise, you may have been impatient as a child, and overreacted quickly to events, and so you want to become more patient.

Living Your Values

Once you've identified your core values, prioritise them in order of importance. Stay connected to them, check in regularly, and ensure your goals and daily actions reflect what matters most.

It can also be powerful to focus on one value per day. For example, if health is a core value, you might choose to drink more water, eat nourishing foods, or take a mindful walk. Small daily actions reinforce your values and keep you aligned.

> For a step-by-step guide to elicit your values, and an extensive list of core values,
> visit the **REWIRE Resources Portal**.

STRENGTHS AND TALENTS

We all possess natural strengths and talents, yet because they come so easily, we often overlook them. Instead, our minds tend to focus on our weaknesses, what's not going well, due to our built-in negativity bias.

In my coaching programs, I often ask clients to list five strengths and five weaknesses. I'm always amazed at how most people can quickly rattle off their weaknesses, yet struggle to name their strengths. Sound familiar? It's often because we've been raised to believe that listing our strengths is some kind of bragging, while admitting our weaknesses is some kind of humility.

But here's the truth. Knowing your strengths is a game-changer. It builds self-belief, confidence, and resilience, key ingredients of a high-performance mindset. It's absolutely not bragging if you're honest about it and don't exaggerate your strengths, simply stating the truth about you. When you understand and lean into your strengths, you overcome doubt, or imposter syndrome, make better decisions, and feel more empowered to take actions that align with your goals.

DISCOVERING YOUR STRENGTHS

Strengths Timeline Reflection

One of my favourite exercises I created to help my clients identify their strengths is the Strengths Timeline Reflection. It's a fun and insightful way to look at your past and recognise the qualities that have helped you grow.

- **Create a Timeline.**
  Draw a horizontal line on a piece of paper, dividing it into five-year blocks.

- **Document Key Events.**
  Below the line, write down significant moments, challenges, or turning points from each time period.

- **Identify Your Strengths.**
  Above the line, note the strengths you relied on or developed during those experiences.

NOTE: This exercise is designed to focus on positive or neutral experiences. Avoid deeply painful memories unless you can reflect objectively and curiously on them and identify one or more key strengths you developed as a result of getting through these experiences.

Here is an example from my own timeline:

- Discovered a love for horse riding and had to fund half my lessons.
  Strengths:
  Resourcefulness
  (I sold produce, mowed lawns, cleaned cars, and vacuumed floors to pay for lessons.)

- Left school and pursued further education at college.
  Strengths:
  Independence and Determination

- Moved to a new city for university.
  Strengths:
  Courage and Curiosity to explore and try new things

- Travelled to the U.S. to teach horse riding at a summer camp.
  Strengths:
  Self-Belief, Passion and Adventurous Spirit

- Embarked on solo adventures around the globe.
  Strengths:
  Independence, Grit, Courage and Determination

Reflecting on your journey like this highlights patterns in your strengths, showing you what has been driving your success all along. It also helps you see how far you have grown. Once you know them, and have logged them, you can intentionally lean on them to face future challenges with confidence.

> You can download a copy of this technique in the **REWIRE Resources Portal**.

Get Feedback from Others

Another way to gain insight is by asking people you trust how they perceive your strengths. Be selective about whom you ask, and stay open to their feedback. Sometimes, others see strengths in us that we take for granted. Finally, taking profile tests is a great way to discover more about yourself. I will delve into a few of my favourites in Chapter 8, Impact.

CLARITY TO CONSISTENCY TO IMPACT

Understanding your values and strengths gives you the clarity to know who you are and what matters most. But clarity alone isn't enough, success comes from taking consistent action.

The more you align your habits with your values and strengths, the easier it becomes to stay consistent. And consistency is the key that unlocks long-term success.

In the next chapter, we will explore how to create consistency, maintain momentum, and keep showing up even when motivation fades.

Because when you consistently take aligned action, that's when you create real impact, in your life, your work, and the world around you.

FINAL THOUGHTS

As Aristotle said:

---

*"Knowing yourself
is the beginning of all wisdom."*

When you gain clarity on who you are, your values, strengths, and what truly matters, you create a solid foundation for a high-performance mindset. This clarity fuels confidence, sharpens your focus, and helps you take action with intention.

The more you understand yourself from the inside out, the more empowered you become. The next step? Turning clarity into consistency, because success isn't about what you do once; it's about what you do repeatedly.

KEY INSIGHTS

- ✓ **Clear goals** give you direction and purpose.
- ✓ **Feeling the emotions of your goals** as already achieved makes them more familiar and real.
- ✓ **Visualisation** helps rewire your brain, reinforcing new beliefs and behaviours.
- ✓ **The better you know yourself,** your values, strengths, and drivers, the more confidence and empowerment you gain.

ACTION STEPS

- **Create a clear 12-month vision for where you want to be.**
  Set 2-5 meaningful goals using the CLEARer Goals Method to ensure clarity and alignment.
- **Align your goals** with your values to stay motivated and fulfilled.
- **Observe and reshape unhelpful thoughts,** replacing them with empowering ones.
- **Identify and leverage your strengths** to build confidence and self-belief.

By taking these steps, you're not just setting goals, you're building the mindset, habits, and inner foundation that will drive long-term success. Now, let's move forward to consistency, the key to creating habits and making it all stick.

CHAPTER 7:
Developing Consistency

*"We are what we repeatedly do.
Excellence, then, is not an act, but a habit."*

— WILL DURANT

Consistency is the cornerstone of success. It's about sustained, purposeful actions that accumulate over time to create meaningful change. Whether forming habits, managing thoughts, or elevating emotions, consistency ensures we follow through on the intentions that lead to lasting transformation. Furthermore, being consistent is necessary to rewire your brain, change, and create a new future.

HABITS: THE FOUNDATION OF SUCCESS

"95% of who you are by the age of 35 is a memorised set of behaviours, emotional reactions, unconscious habits, and beliefs."

— DR JOE DISPENZA

A habit is a behaviour that is repeated so often it has become automatic, consequently, we often do them without thinking about them. Habits are formed from daily routines and rituals, triggered by specific cues. To build a habit, you need to repeat a particular routine over multiple occasions, experiencing a positive feeling each time. In other words, the habitual behaviour evokes or satisfies some kind of reward in the brain.

A new habit can take days, weeks, or even months to form. Habits are stored in the brain's basal ganglia, which connect actions to rewards, and once created, become automatic and are run in our subconscious mind. Once formed, they require relatively little brain power to carry out. They happen automatically, and they free up mental energy for other things. The key to effective habit-building lies in repetition, positive reinforcement, and alignment with our goals.

As we operate most of our day by habit, they are the foundation of our success and shape our identity, how we show up and what we do.

Moreover, we need to work on developing mental and emotional habits as well as physical habits; a key to rewire our brains and achieve the success we desire.

THE POWER OF HABITS

Charles Duhigg, author of *The Power of Habits* says this about habits:

"Habits are powerful, but delicate.
They can emerge outside our consciousness or
can be deliberately designed.
They often occur without our permission,
but can be reshaped by fiddling with their parts.
Habits shape our lives far more than we realise
— they are so strong, in fact, that they cause
our brains to cling to them at the exclusion of all
else, including common sense."

Ultimately, habits are neither good nor bad. It's how well they serve you.

It's when we are stressed or tired that our habits come into play, which makes observing ourselves in such situations a key to determine whether they are helpful or a hindrance to our success.

When we experience a threat, our rational, conscious decision-making processes tend to shut down, although this is when we most need our full brainpower. As it's less available, we tend to operate from the behaviour that requires the least effort. If we have habits that align with our goals, values and intentions, then even under pressure they help us respond at our best. They raise us up rather than bringing us down; help us feel safe, familiar, and act predictably.

However, the automaticity of habits has an upside and a downside. When our habits are not aligned with our goals, they get in our way. Given that something like 43%, as a minimum, of our behaviour is habitual, we have plenty of scope for self-examination and improving our habits.

THE SCIENCE OF HABITS

Charles Duhigg, in his book, also explains that there is a science to habits, and they follow a predictable "habit loop" consisting of three components:

- **Cue:** A trigger that initiates the behaviour.
- **Routine:** The behaviour itself.
- **Reward:** The positive reinforcement that solidifies the habit.

For example, if your goal is to plan your day, the cue might be turning on your computer, the routine is creating your plan, and the reward is feeling accomplished and in control. If you have a poor habit of snacking after you get home from work, the cue may be walking into the kitchen after work, the routine is opening the fridge to look for food, and the reward is a feeling of relaxation or entitlement after a hard day.

Tips for Creating Habits: Small Steps and Small Improvements

When you are starting to develop a habit, the goal is to build momentum by getting some early wins on the board. The key, therefore, is to start small and keep it achievable. For example, if you want to run a half-marathon but have never ran one before, start with a walk-run twice a week. When you are consistent, you can increase the intensity and duration of the run. It can also be helpful to make small improvements in different areas of your life rather than trying to radically change one thing, such as giving up all unhealthy food, snacking, alcohol, chocolate all at once.

A great example of small improvements in many areas comes from David Brailsford, coach of Team Sky, who transformed British cycling. Brailsford emphasised the importance of "marginal gains."

By improving tiny aspects of performance, better sleep, nutrition, and equipment, the cumulative effect led to numerous Olympic medals and Tour de France victories.

This principle can be applied in creating habits:

- **Start small.**
  Schedule the new behaviour so it is manageable and doable.

- **Celebrate small wins.**
  Success builds self-belief, an essential ingredient of a high-performance mindset and your success, as it builds you up at the level of identity.

- **Embrace consistency.**
  Small steps compound, like interest, to create significant results.

THE ROLE OF DOPAMINE AND REWARDS

The reason that celebrating your successes is key is the role of dopamine, the brain's "feel-good" chemical. In relation to habit formation, research by James Olds and Peter Milner shows that dopamine drives motivation and reinforces behaviour. Therefore, if you reward yourself after completing a task, however small, whether with a fist pump, a short break, or a small treat, it helps you keep going, as you feel good about your wins. Additionally, immediate rewards strengthen neural connections, making the behaviour more likely to stick.

Building Willpower: The Five-Minute Rule

Strengthening willpower is essential for forming habits. It helps you delay gratification and resist short-term temptations to achieve long-term goals.

This applies to both actions and thoughts, such as avoiding distractions, negative self-talk, or impulses like reaching for chocolate when you're trying to eat healthy.

To build your will and defer instant gratification, try this simple but effective technique, the Five-Minute Rule:

Instead of giving in to an urge immediately, wait five minutes.

Use this time to find an alternative action that aligns with your goals.

This small act of self-discipline strengthens your willpower over time.

For example, if you're tempted to procrastinate, commit to working for just five minutes. If you want to quit a workout early, push for five more minutes. If you want to have another glass of wine or piece of chocolate, wait five minutes first.

Small acts of resistance build resilience and self-control, making future efforts easier.

Additionally, creating identity-based statements such as *"I'm the sort of person who chooses healthy foods"* or *"I'm the sort of person who easily says no to desserts."*

Finally, as you will read in this book, we must beware of negatives. However, like everything, they have their uses as they can be powerful allies in creating healthy habits. For example, you might choose to say, *"I don't drink during the week,"* or. *"I don't eat desserts,"* or *"I don't sleep in."*

Using the Environment to Your Advantage

The other important area when creating habits is being aware of your environment. It plays a crucial role in shaping your habits, and can both hinder and help you.

Remember, you have the power to control certain elements in your environment. For instance, you can add or remove elements from your surroundings to support positive behaviours.

Remove Distractions and Temptations

To reduce distractions at work and stay focused, turn off notifications and close unnecessary tabs when working.

To avoid snacking, place tempting foods out of sight or in hard-to-reach places.

Add Things to Your Environment

To motivate yourself to exercise in the morning, put your workout clothes by your bed and keep your alarm clock on the other side of the room to help you get out of bed.

If you want to drink more water, place a full water bottle and a glass on your desk.

A powerful example of leveraging a change in the environment comes from Dick Fosbury, who revolutionised the high jump with the "Fosbury Flop."

By using new foam landing mats, he developed an unusual technique that won him Olympic gold, demonstrating that innovation and success come from adapting to one's environment.

Client Story: The Power of Changing Habits

One of my greatest success stories, way back at the beginning of my business, involves Amanda, a business owner who came to work with me. As a single parent running a large family business, she was highly stressed and juggling many responsibilities. To numb her stress and stop it from consuming her thoughts, she smoked, drank daily, and turned to food as a comfort to ease her stress. Additionally, she had a child with special needs, which also gave her extra challenges.

She knew she needed to change, but felt overwhelmed and couldn't do it on her own.

Together we created a plan, prioritising the most important areas to focus on first, and one that involved small steps. First we worked on creating some small and simple morning routines focusing on improving her health. Next she quit smoking, which helped her feel healthier. As she worked more on exercising, she felt more motivated and fitter. Then we focused on cutting down on alcohol, and then she quit alcohol totally. Feeling fitter and more empowered, she increased the intensity and duration of her exercise until it became a healthy habit.

Ultimately, as well as quitting smoking and alcohol, she lost 25 kilograms and embraced exercise and a healthy lifestyle.

Years later, she is still a non-smoker and non-drinker, looks great, and enjoys a happier, thriving life. She has control of her life and her mind. Achieving this required discipline, motivation, a clear plan, consistent effort, kindness, and expert support, to ensure her mindset was positive and help her build the mental strength needed to overcome setbacks along the road to success. Similar to how athletes achieve their success and win gold medals.

"Habits are like the atoms of our lives, each one is a fundamental unit that contributes to your overall improvement."

— JAMES CLEAR

SEVEN KEYS TO SUCCESSFUL HABITS

1. Identify the habit and connect it to your "why."
2. Link it to a bigger goal and create urgency.
3. Start small and set a clear plan.
4. Design your environment to support the habit.
5. Reinforce your identity with positive statements and visualisation.
6. Track your progress and reward your efforts.
7. Reflect regularly with curiosity and kindness.

> For a comprehensive Habit Creation Checklist, visit the **REWIRE Resources Portal**.

One of the key points above is being kind to yourself as you develop your habit. It's not about perfection, but consistency, and picking yourself up, starting again when you fall down.

As Dan Millman says:

*"Compassionate self-awareness
leads to change;
harsh self-criticism only holds
the pattern in place."*

Let's explore the three essential areas for developing good habits. These are necessary for creating a high-performance mindset for excellence.

MENTAL HABITS

Your thoughts are powerful and shape your reality. As you recall from the chapter on Clarity, positive thoughts promote success, while negative ones punish your potential.

Creating Positive Statements to Rewire Your Brain

"The outer conditions of a person's life will always be found to reflect their inner beliefs."

— JAMES ALLEN

In the previous chapter, I shared a technique to help release negative thinking. Building on this, the next step is to create helpful and positive habits of thought. I teach my clients to create POSTs (Positive Statements), which are simple yet powerful statements that help them become who they want to be or enhance their skills.

For instance:

Instead of saying, *"I am supremely confident,"* try: *"Every day, I am becoming even more confident."*

To learn more effectively, *"Every day, I effortlessly learn one new thing"*.

Additionally, you can create identity statements, or POISTs, (Positive Identity Statements) as above: "I'm the sort of person who always embraces morning exercise."

To embed these into your subconscious and help rewire your thoughts:

- Write them down.
- Repeat them daily.
- Attach a positive emotion to them while repeating them.
- Visualise yourself having achieved your outcome.

These steps engage your senses: sight, sound, and feeling, to help embed new thoughts in your subconscious mind and rewire your thinking patterns to create naturally positive habits of thought.

Just as a seed holds the potential for growth, so do your thoughts. Whether you plant a weed or a flower, your brain will respond accordingly. Plant a weed, and toxic thoughts will take root. Plant a flower, and growth and positivity will flourish. Remember, everything starts with a thought. Your life, success, and future depend on managing your mind and cultivating habits that support growth and self-belief.

Consistency in mental habits is just as crucial as consistency in physical habits, and science backs this up. Norman Doidge in *The Brain That Changes Itself*, highlights the power of repetition and pruning in brain development. *"Neurons that fire together, wire together,"* while unused neural connections weaken and disappear.

This means that by focusing on positive thoughts and consciously releasing or ignoring negative ones, you are literally reshaping your brain for success. It is also fundamental to cultivating a high-performance mindset.

Jan came to me after a difficult chapter in her life. She was recovering from cancer, emotionally depleted, and burdened by fear and overwhelm. She arrived at our first session carrying not only her thoughts, but a literal bag packed "just in case" her anxiety triggered physical symptoms.
Together, we worked on gently releasing old thought patterns and creating new ones using POSTs — Positive Statements. Through daily repetition, visualisation, and anchoring new thoughts to emotion, Jan gradually began to shift her inner dialogue and rewire her brain, creating a new, more empowered story.

Over time, her energy lifted, her confidence returned, and most importantly, she started to feel like herself again. *"I've learned to recognise 'me', and who and what I am. I have reached my goal of happiness and wellbeing and feel good about myself. I can be me without fear of what others think. Life is good,"* she told me.

Her story reminds us that even in our darkest moments, small shifts in thought can create powerful change.

To access an infographic on how to create POSTs, visit the **REWIRE Resources Portal**.

The Habit of Visualisation

*"When you visualize, then you materialize.
If you've been there in the mind,
you'll go there in the body."*

— DR. DENIS WAITLEY

In the preceding chapter, I discussed visualising yourself having achieved your vision and goals. Now, it's time to take this one step further by consciously practicing mental rehearsal to enhance your performance.

Mental rehearsal is a powerful cognitive tool used by top athletes and high achievers. Jack Nicklaus, Michael Phelps, and many others attribute their success to visualising perfect outcomes before they happen. During my training for the Australian Ironman Championships in Forster, I imagined myself swimming, exiting the water, transitioning to the bike, cycling the course, and running the marathon. Most importantly, I imagined myself crossing the finish line numerous times, seeing a finishing time that would result in my qualifying for the Ironman World Championships in Kona, embracing the moment of success.

This nightly practice prepared my mind and body for success, and on race day, when I crossed the finish line, I did a time of 10 hours 44 minutes, good enough to achieve my dream and qualify for the Hawaiian Ironman.

Michael Phelps' coach, Bob Bowman, implemented a specific mental habit known as 'the videotape' to prepare him for competition.

Each night before bed and every morning, Phelps would mentally rehearse his perfect race, every stroke, turn, and every detail down to the feel of the water dripping off his lips at the finish.

By the time he competed, his mind had already experienced success, reinforcing his confidence and execution.

Specific experiments also give the same results. Years ago, an experiment was conducted on the effects of mental practice on improving skill in sinking basketball free throws. One group of students practised throwing the ball every day for 20 days and were scored on the first and last days. A second group was scored on the first and last days and engaged in no practice at all in between. A third group was scored on the first day, then spent 20 minutes a day imagining that they were throwing the ball at the goal. When they missed, they would imagine that they had corrected their aim accordingly. The first group, which practised 20 minutes every day, improved their scoring by 24%. The second group, which had no sort of practice, not surprisingly, showed no improvement. The third group, which practised only in their imagination, improved their scoring by 23%.

This shows that mental rehearsal can be as effective as real-world repetition. When you combine physical training and mental rehearsal, you have a great winning combination.

The reason why visualisation and specific mental rehearsal work is because your brain doesn't distinguish between real and imagined experiences. Vividly imagining an event activates the same brain pathways as real experiences.

This strengthens those neural connections, making it easier to perform the action in reality. Moreover, you are programming your Reticular Activating System to search for what you are visualising.

> *"Human beings always act, and feel, and perform in accordance with what they imagine to be true about themselves and their environment."*
>
> — MAXWELL MALTZ

How to Practice Mental Rehearsal

Step 1:
Create a Clear Mental Picture
Imagine yourself having achieved your goal. Picture the details as vividly as possible; where you are, what you see, hear, and feel.

Step 2:
Engage All Your Senses
Feel the confidence of delivering a speech successfully, the rush of crossing a marathon finish line, or the excitement of securing a big business deal. The more sensory detail you add, the more real it becomes to your brain.

Step 3:
See Yourself 'In the Moment of the Wish Fulfilled'
As Neville Goddard teaches, stand in the moment of achievement, experiencing the emotions of success as if it has already

happened. This aligns your mindset, beliefs, and actions toward making it a reality.

Step 4:
Repeat Daily
The more frequently you practice mental rehearsal, the stronger the neural pathways become. With time, visualisation turns intention into expectation, reinforcing your ability to execute successfully.

When you have mastered the basics, you can start to do what Michael Phelps did and visualise yourself overcoming obstacles and challenges, to lock in strategies and become more adept when the event happens.

By incorporating visualisation into your daily routine, you train your brain for success, enhance confidence, and rewire your brain for greater performances.

Limiting Beliefs: Uncovering and Replacing Blocks

"Your beliefs become your thoughts,
your thoughts become your words,
your words become your actions,
your actions become your habits,
your habits become your values,
your values become your destiny."

— MAHATMA GANDHI

I've talked about the power of words and the importance of using them to help build self-belief. A massive step forward (and true transformation) happens when we identify and clear our limiting beliefs. Many of the beliefs that shape our lives today were formed in childhood, before we reached the age of nine. A scary thought. This means they act as powerful yet invisible barriers to our success.

These beliefs become deeply embedded in our subconscious, shaping our decisions, behaviours, and the way we see ourselves. Moreover, our brain seeks to confirm and bring into reality what it already believes. It focuses on what it knows; the well-established, existing programs. Unless we identify and clear our limiting beliefs. Our outcomes will only be dictated by the patterns the brain already knows.

Some common examples of limiting beliefs include:

- *"I'm not good enough."*
- *"Success is for others, not me."*
- *"I don't have the time or resources."*

Dissolving Limiting Beliefs

Here's a powerful way to identify and break free from limiting beliefs. Questions shift your awareness and energy around beliefs, helping you reframe their meaning.

Run each belief through the following ten questions:

- Where did this belief originate?

- Is it true for everyone?
- Do I truly believe it, or have I accepted it without question?
- What's the payoff for holding onto this belief?
- What has this belief cost me?
- What opportunities has it prevented?
- What specific, positive changes would occur if I released it?
- How do these potential results feel?
- What new belief could replace this one?
- What actions or habits will help embed this new belief?

Once you've identified a new, empowering belief, write it down. Then, turn it into a POST (Positive Statement) and repeat it daily. This repetition strengthens neural pathways, gradually replacing the old belief with the new one.

For example, if you discover a belief like *"I'm not good enough"* and work through the questions, you begin to shift the energy of it, and your perspective. You then create a new, empowering belief: *"I am worthy and capable enough to achieve whatever I set my mind to."*

Next, reinforce this belief with a POST to help embed it into your subconscious mind so it becomes part of your identity.

"Every day I believe in myself more, as new opportunities show up for me."

Remember, your Reticular Activating System seeks to bring into your reality what you program it with, so once you focus on this new belief, you'll start noticing more moments where you experience moments where you feel capable, receive praise, or attract opportunities.

Additionally, action builds belief. Taking small, aligned steps reinforces the truth that change is possible. For instance, if you see an opportunity to attend a workshop and decide to enrol, that action strengthens your new belief in yourself.

In the above example, perhaps you see an opportunity to attend a workshop and you decide to enrol.

Rewiring your mind takes time, commitment, and self-kindness, but with consistency, you can shift old patterns and create a new reality.

> Access a copy of the questions to dissolve limiting beliefs in the **REWIRE Resources Portal**.

EMOTIONAL HABITS

Positive emotions are a key to a healthier, happier life and a driver of high performance. They help build belief, fuel mental toughness, or grit, and expand your energy into the realm of possibility. When we cultivate positive emotional states consistently, we rewire our brains for success and potential.

Boosting Immune Function Through Elevated Emotions

Dr. Joe Dispenza's research highlights the profound impact of elevated emotions like gratitude and joy, showing that they not only enhance well-being but can also influence gene expression.

He conducted a compelling study demonstrating the physiological effects of positive emotions, attention, and meditation. In this experiment, 120 participants practised feeling elevated emotions, such as love, joy, or gratitude, for just nine to ten minutes, three times a day, for four days.

The question was this. If, by elevating their emotional state, would they decrease cortisol levels and increase their levels of immunoglobulin A (IgA), thereby naturally boosting their immune system?

The results were a resounding yes.

Cortisol levels (the stress hormone) decreased significantly.

Levels of immunoglobulin A (IgA), a key immune-boosting antibody, increased by 49.5%.

This study underscores a powerful truth: your emotional state directly affects your physical health. By cultivating emotions that serve you, you create a foundation for long-term success, well-being, and resilience. Additionally, your energy ripples out and positively influences and impacts the world around you. All of this helps you build a high-performance mindset.

Just as you've learned the importance of observing your thoughts, you must start observing your emotions. Where do you feel them in your body? How do they shift throughout the day? Can you name them? This helps build self-awareness — the first step in learning to respond to emotions rather than reacting in your old, habitual way.

Now, let's explore three powerful techniques to elevate your emotional state and build positive emotional habits.

Gratitude: Rewiring Your Brain for Positivity

"Wear gratitude like a cloak, and it will feed every corner of your life."

— Rumi

Gratitude is one of the most powerful emotional habits you can cultivate. It shifts your focus from what's lacking to what's abundant, rewiring your brain for positivity and enhancing overall well-being. Neuroscience shows that expressing gratitude activates reward centres in the brain, reinforcing positive emotions and helping you break free from habitual negativity.

Dr. Joe Dispenza's research highlights how gratitude can even influence gene expression. In one of his retreats, a participant named Angelia used gratitude as a tool for healing. By consistently feeling grateful for her recovery before it had even occurred, she sent a powerful message to her body, activating the biological processes that supported her healing.

This demonstrates a key principle of neuroplasticity: the brain can't tell the difference between what's real and vividly imagined, which is why visualisation and positive emotions are so effective.

When you practice gratitude as if the positive outcome has already happened, your body and mind align with that reality.

Starting a Gratitude Journal

One of the simplest yet most effective ways to cultivate gratitude is by keeping a daily gratitude journal. This habit helps rewire your brain to focus on the positive, counteracting the mind's natural negativity bias. As it can take around five positive thoughts to neutralise a negative thought, the more you concentrate on the good, the stronger your positive mindset and optimistic attitude become.

"Acknowledging the good that you already have in your life is the foundation for all abundance."

— ECKHART TOLLE

How to Start:

- **Set aside a few minutes each day.**
  Ideally, write in your journal first thing in the morning or before bed.

- **List at least three things you're grateful for.**
  These can be small joys or significant events.

- **Be specific.**
  Instead of *"I'm grateful for my job,"* try *"I'm grateful for the supportive conversation I had with my colleague today."*

- **Feel the gratitude.**
  As you write, take a moment to deeply appreciate each journal item.

Examples:

- *I'm grateful for the warmth of the sun on my face during my morning walk.*
- *I'm grateful to my friend who checked in on me today; I feel valued.*
- *I'm grateful for the delicious home-cooked meal I enjoyed with my family.*

With repetition, this simple practice strengthens neural pathways associated with optimism and resilience.

Client Story: The Shift from Stress to Gratitude

Kate, a corporate executive, was constantly overwhelmed by work pressures. She found herself stuck in a cycle of stress, always focusing on what wasn't working rather than what was. Through coaching, she committed to a daily gratitude practice, writing down three things she was grateful for every evening.

At first, she struggled to do it consistently. But after a few weeks, Kate noticed a shift. Instead of dwelling on frustrations, she began to naturally seek out moments of appreciation during her day.

The more she trained her mind to recognise the good, the more her stress levels decreased. Within a few months, she reported feeling lighter, more focused, and even sleeping better.

Gratitude didn't change Kate's workload, but it transformed her perspective. It gave her more energy and resilience to handle challenges effectively. Moreover, it helped her focus on her successes and be more present, instead of worrying about what she hadn't achieved.

By making gratitude a daily habit, you can train your brain to shift from scarcity to abundance and positivity.

This small yet profound shift can significantly impact your mindset, your physical health, and your happiness.

Amplifying Positive Emotions

The following technique is a simple yet transformative beginning, or end-of-day practice that not only strengthens confidence but also elevates your emotional state, which is crucial for success.

Spend a few minutes each morning or each night focusing on a happy memory or envisioning a joyful future event. Doing this consistently will elevate your mood, increase resilience, and help rewire your brain for positivity.

To enhance this effect, combine the practice with calm, conscious breathing. Conscious breathing calms the nervous system, allowing positive emotions to take root more deeply.

It also ties back to an earlier point, just 0.1 per cent of the square root of a population practicing a focused intention can create measurable change in the surrounding environment. This reinforces the idea that small, intentional actions, like gratitude, can have a profound ripple effect in your life and results, too.

> *"A positive state of mind is not merely good for you; it benefits everyone with whom you come into contact, literally changing the world."*
>
> — DALAI LAMA

Self-Appreciation: Elevating Your Emotions Through Inner Wins

This technique includes two additional steps; both designed to support a third, powerful step, that helps build self-belief and confidence by working at the level of identity.

1. **Write down three small wins from your day.**
   They don't have to be major achievements. Simple things such as completing a workout, handling a tough conversation well, making a healthy lunch, or completing a small task, count.

2. **Now, turn the lens inward.**
   Identify the strength, talent, or trait within you that made each win possible. Did you show resilience, creativity, curiosity, patience, or determination?

3. **Feel appreciation for yourself.**
   Most people easily recognise their weaknesses due to our brain's negativity bias, so this exercise helps you shift your

focus to what you do well. In essence, you are being your own best champion, so this exercise shifts your focus to what you do well, creating a positive emotional state.

By practising self-appreciation and focusing on your strengths, you feel good about yourself, reinforcing feelings of self-worth and empowerment. Yet another tool to help rewire your mindset faster, build self-belief, and take charge of your future.

> To deepen this habit, download the Self-Appreciation Exercise PDF from the **REWIRE Resources section**.

PHYSICAL HABITS

"Action may not always bring happiness, but there is no happiness without action."

— BENJAMIN DISRAELI

Starting Your Day the Right Way

The way you start your day sets the tone for your focus, energy, and productivity. If you wake up feeling overwhelmed by your to-do list or work deadlines, your brain shifts into reactive mode, leading to stress-driven decisions. Often, this results in choosing quick, easy tasks over meaningful, high-impact work.

We are wired to seek pleasure and avoid pain, which is why checking emails or scrolling social media feels easier than tackling a challenging task. However, these habits quickly drain your mental energy and destroy productivity.

Instead, start your day with intention by focusing on three key areas:

1. **Mental:**
   Set a clear intention for the day, visualising how you want to feel once your key goal is accomplished.

2. **Emotional:**
   Practice gratitude or recall a positive moment to elevate your emotional state.

3. **Physical:**
   Move your body, whether through stretching, walking, or a workout, to activate energy and focus.

I call these the bookends, the habits that frame the beginning and end of your day. By establishing a solid morning routine, you create momentum and clarity, setting yourself up for success.

"A champion doesn't become a champion in the ring; he is merely recognized there. His becoming happens during his daily routine."

— WILL DURANT

Energy Management: Push and Recovery

Sustaining peak performance isn't about constantly pushing yourself, it's about balancing effort and recovery. Without proper energy management, fatigue sets in, making it harder to maintain consistency.

Tony Schwartz, author of *The Power of Full Engagement*, emphasises:

> *"Human beings are not machines. We're designed to pulse, moving between spending and renewing energy."*

Balanced Breathing

One of the simplest ways to reset your energy is through mindful breathing. Take two minutes to shift your focus to your breath, allowing your mind to reset and your body to relax. Because the heart regulates the autonomic nervous system, when your breathing is slow and steady, your heart becomes coherent. When your heart is coherent, you are literally giving your nervous system a break. Additionally, when your heart is coherent, your brain is coherent, which helps enhance mental clarity, increase focus and reduce stress. Practising this throughout the day at regular intervals is a great way to maintain calm and look after your wellbeing.

> You can access this technique in the **REWIRE Resources Portal**.

Take Short Breaks to Renew Energy

Research shows that taking regular breaks, especially movement-based or mindful pauses, helps maintain focus, creativity, and productivity throughout the day, and reduces the need for a long recovery at the end of the day.

We'll explore more advanced energy management strategies in the next chapter on Impact.

Reflection: Learning and Growth

A powerful end-of-day habit, the second bookend of your day, is reflection. Taking a few minutes to pause and consciously reflect on your day helps build awareness and gain insights. Insights are essential for learning, growing, and shaping your future, allowing you to adjust your approach as required.

James Bailey states:

> *"Reflection is the foundation from which all other soft skills grow."*

To make reflection a simple, effective habit, ask yourself these seven daily questions:

- What did I do well today?
- What did I learn?
- What could I have done better?
- What was my biggest time waster?
- What am I grateful for?
- What was the most impactful moment of my day?
- What will I commit to doing tomorrow?

FINAL THOUGHTS

Consistency isn't about perfection. It's about showing up daily, taking small steps, and embracing curiosity and kindness along the way. By mastering your mental, emotional and physical habits, you rewire your brain, cultivate a high-performance mindset, and achieve lasting transformation.

KEY INSIGHTS

- ✓ **Habits** are the foundation of success.
- ✓ ***"Neurons that fire together, wire together."*** Repetition helps embed new patterns.
- ✓ **Elevated emotions** help you feel good, build resilience and enhance high performance.

ACTION STEPS

- **Choose one mental habit and commit to doing it daily** (e.g., a daily affirmation or positive statement, POST).

- **Embrace one technique to work on your emotional state** (e.g., gratitude journaling or amplifying positive emotions).

- **Decide on one physical habit** (e.g., a morning walk, planning your day, or other structured routine.)

- **Repeat daily** to help build habits in all three areas and transform your results.

By combining clarity with consistency, you create the foundation for greater impact, both in your own life and in the lives of those around you. In the next chapter, we'll explore how to leverage this momentum, break through limitations, and cultivate additional habits that lead to lasting excellence.

CHAPTER 8:
Creating Impact

"Example is not the main thing in influencing others. It is the only thing."

— ALBERT SCHWEITZER

Impact isn't just about what you do, it's about who you are when no one is watching. It's about the small, daily choices that shape your future, the energy and intentionality you bring to every situation, and the way you consistently show up in the world.

How you do one thing is a reflection of how you do many things.

In this chapter, we'll explore six key strategies to strengthen your mindset, elevate your performance, and create real impact. By integrating what you've learned about clarity and consistency, you will refine your focus, sharpen your attention, and optimise your energy, allowing you to be at your best when it matters most.

CORE ENERGY

> *"When you are inspired by some great purpose... dormant forces, faculties and talents become alive."*
>
> — PATANJALI

At the heart of your ability to create impact is your Core Energy. This is the force that is behind everything you do. But Core Energy isn't just about stamina or drive; it's an extension of your identity.

Who you are at your core, your beliefs, mindset, and values shape your actions, habits, and ultimately, your ability to create meaningful impact.

When you know who you are; when your identity is clear and aligned, your energy flows freely. You exude confidence, feel stronger, empowered, and have a greater level of self-belief. If you're not aligned and don't follow through on your commitments, your energy will be lower and more scattered. You will feel less confident, lack momentum, and others will pick up on your energy.

Think of your core energy like the engine of a high-performance sports car. One that delivers speed, precision, and great performance. But if that engine is neglected or misaligned, performance suffers. Your core energy works the same way. To create lasting impact, you must fuel, care for, and fine-tune your mental, emotional, and physical energy.

To perform at your best, managing your energy is just as important, if not more so, than managing your time. You can't show up as your best self when you're mentally drained, emotionally scattered, or physically exhausted. That's why the REWIRE Model places a strong emphasis on energy alignment.

To optimise your core energy:

- Strengthen your self-awareness and learn to identify and eliminate energy drainers, and enhance energy elevators.
- Ensure your thoughts, beliefs, values, and behaviours align with your goals.
- Master the art of emotional regulation, your energy is shaped by your emotions.
- Develop recovery strategies. Energy isn't infinite; it must be replenished.

THRIVING IN A FAST-MOVING WORLD

"In times of change learners inherit the earth; while the learned find themselves beautifully equipped to deal with a world that no longer exists."

— ERIC HOFFER

Adaptability is a non-negotiable skill in today's fast-changing world. High performers do not fear change; they lean into it, recognising that what worked yesterday may not work tomorrow.

British psychiatrist and cybernetician Ross Ashby introduced the *Law of Requisite Variety*, which states that to effectively navigate complexity, a system must have an equal variety of responses. In other words, the more unpredictable your environment, the more adaptable you must be to thrive. Those who resist change risk falling behind, while those who embrace it unlock new levels of success.

History has shown that those who anticipate and respond to shifts in the landscape are the ones who thrive. Consider the pace of technological advancements: Ford Motor Company took almost 50 years to reach one billion users, while Google achieved this in less than six years. Companies like Airbnb, Uber, Canva, and Atlassian revolutionised industries by recognising trends early and adapting swiftly.

The same principle applies to individuals. To stay impactful, we must continually refine our skills, rethink old perspectives, and embrace new opportunities.

The 1990s saw a surge in the popularity of triathlons, driven by the growth of high-profile events like the Ironman World Championship in Hawaii and the sport's inclusion in the Olympic Games for Sydney 2000.

During this time, I discovered triathlons, initially drawn to them as a great way to stay fit, and later as a challenge to push my limits. Back then, the prevailing belief in elite circles was that more training always led to better performance. Athletes followed gruelling training programs, often pushing their bodies beyond their limits without fully understanding the long-term health consequences.

Over time, however, the risks of overtraining became clear. Some of the sport's greatest triathletes, including Greg Welch and Emma Carney, saw their careers cut short due to heart conditions. Even my former training partner, Peter, suffered major heart damage. These cases reinforced an important lesson: relentless effort alone is not the key to sustained success.

Today, a smarter, science-backed approach prevails. Take Australian swimmer Cameron McEvoy, a four-time Olympian, who revolutionised his training by embracing a physics-based model. He reduced pool time in favour of strength training, a strategy that led him to a world championship victory in 2023 and set him on track for the 2024 Paris Olympics and beyond.

His success highlights key ingredients of a high-performance mindset: embracing change, challenging conventional methods, and finding innovative solutions to continually improve and stay ahead.

Whether you are in business, sport or personal growth, those who adapt thrive. Those who resist change get left behind.

We must ask better questions, ones that spark curiosity and open new possibilities:

- *"How can I adjust my approach?"*
- *"What opportunities does this shift create?"*
- *"What else could happen as a result of this shift?"*

By embracing adaptability, you do not just survive change, you thrive in it.

THE POWER OF DELIBERATE, PURPOSEFUL PRACTICE

*"The brain changes with practice.
You cannot do just one thing, one time, and
rewire your brain for success."*

— JOHN ARDEN

Adapting to change is only the first step. To truly excel, you must take intentional action to refine your skills and elevate your performance. High performers don't just react to change, they actively shape their future through disciplined, focused practice.

Mastery does not happen by accident. High performance is built through deliberate, purposeful practice, not mindless repetition, but structured, intentional effort designed for continuous improvement. This is what separates those who achieve excellence from those who plateau.

Dr. Eddie O'Connor, a sports psychologist, highlights that high-performers practice with intense focus, clear goals, and continual challenges. This method of practice applies across all fields, from elite sports to business and personal development.

How to Practice Deliberately:

- **Set clear, specific goals for each session.**
  Define what success looks like before you begin.

- **Stay fully engaged and focused.**
  Minimise distractions and be intentional with your practice

- **Step outside your comfort zone.**
  Push yourself beyond what feels easy or familiar.

- **Seek expert feedback and adjust.**
  Growth comes from refining your approach based on insights from others.

As Anders Ericsson, author of Peak, said:

*"Practice isn't what you do once
you're good at something.
It's deliberate, purposeful practice
when you're starting out that counts."*

Even the world's greatest athletes rely on this principle. Tennis champion Rafael Nadal summed it up perfectly:

> *"One lesson I've learned is that if the job I do were easy, I wouldn't derive so much satisfaction from it. The thrill of winning is in direct proportion to the effort I put in before. I also know, from long experience, that if you make an effort in training when you don't especially feel like making it, the payoff is that you will win games when you are not feeling your best. That is how you win championships, that is what separates the great player from the merely good player. The difference lies in how well you've prepared."*
>
> — RAFAEL NADAL

How This Applies in Business

Athletes aren't the only ones who benefit from structured, intentional practice. The same principles apply in business, leadership, and any high-performance field. Consider a sales team refining their pitch. Instead of just making calls and hoping for the best, they practice deliberately.

- They role-play difficult conversations before meeting with clients.
- They review call recordings to refine their delivery.
- They seek expert feedback from top performers and coaches.

- They continuously adjust their approach based on data and client responses.

The result? Higher conversion rates, increased confidence, and stronger communication skills. Just like in sports, business success is not about working harder, it's about practicing smarter

Mastery Is a Process, not a Destination

Mastery is not just about repeating a skill, it physically rewires the brain. Neuroscientists have found that individuals who develop skills over time alter their brain structures. For example:

- Divers have more grey matter in regions that control movement.
- Musicians have a larger cerebellum for coordination.
- London taxi drivers have a larger hippocampus.

Mastery is not fixed. It is built through consistent, focused effort over time.

SMALL IMPROVEMENTS, BIG RESULTS

Deliberate, purposeful practice creates the foundation for mastery, but true excellence is built through continuous refinement. Seven-time Olympic medallist Andrew Hoy is a prime example. After decades of competition at the highest level, Hoy no longer needed drastic reinventions; instead, he refined his performance through small, consistent improvements in technique, strategy, and mindset.

> *"If I improve 10 things by one percent, that's a 10 percent increase."*
>
> — ANDREW HOY

At this stage in his career, Hoy's focus was not on making sweeping changes but on marginal gains, fine-tuning the details that could elevate his performance. This philosophy aligns with what British cycling coach Sir Dave Brailsford calls the *"aggregation of marginal gains"*, the idea that small, 1% improvements, when compounded over time, lead to extraordinary results.

The same principle applies to business, leadership, and personal growth. High performers don't just work hard; they work smart, focusing on consistent, intentional refinements that compound into long-term success.

THE ESSENTIAL ROLE OF FEEDBACK

> *"Without feedback — either from yourself or from outside observers — you cannot figure out what you need to improve on or how close you are to achieving your goals."*
>
> — ANDERS ERICSSON, PEAK

One of the most overlooked yet critical components of deliberate practice is feedback. Athletes make minute adjustments that can mean the difference between a gold and a silver medal. The cycle of focus, feedback, and fix is fundamental to continuous improvement.

However, many people resist feedback, taking it as personal criticism rather than constructive insight.

This is where a principle from *The Four Agreements* by Don Miguel Ruiz is invaluable:

> *"Don't take anything personally."*

Feedback is an opportunity to grow, not an attack on your worth.

To win, and to create great performances, you must challenge old patterns, refine your approach, and remain open to learning.

In the words of Marshall Goldsmith:

> *"What got you here, won't get you there."*

THE POWER OF EXPECTATION

"Whether you think you can or think you can't, you're right."

— HENRY FORD

Mastery is not just about refining skills; it is also about shaping the mindset that drives those skills forward. Even with deliberate practice and incremental improvements, your belief in what is possible determines how far you go.

The world's top performers don't just train harder, they expect more from themselves. They understand that expectations influence reality, so they build a strong belief in their ability to improve, overcome obstacles, and achieve extraordinary results.

What you expect of yourself influences how you show up, the actions you take, and ultimately, the results you achieve.

An expectation is more than a passing thought; it is a strong belief that something will happen. When you expect success, you naturally align your actions, decisions, and energy toward achieving it. But when doubt creeps in, it undermines your confidence, keeping you stuck in hesitation and limitations.

A powerful example of expectation at play comes from Eliud Kipchoge, the first person to run a marathon in under two hours. He didn't just train his body; he trained his mind to believe it was possible. His mantra, *"No Human Is Limited,"* became a guiding principle, not just for himself but for the world. He expected to break the barrier, and he did.

This same principle was demonstrated in a well-known study by psychologists Rosenthal and Jacobson. Teachers were told that certain students had high potential, but in reality, the students were randomly selected. Yet by the end of the year, those students had significantly improved. Why? Because expectation influences behaviour. When the teachers believed in the students' potential, they treated them differently, offering more encouragement, guidance, and belief.

The same applies to you. When you raise your expectations, you show up differently. You take bolder actions, make stronger decisions, and push through challenges with confidence. The key is to expect the best, but without attachment to the outcome. Believe in success, act with certainty and clear intention, and trust the process.

As Kipchoge says:

_____

*"The mind is what drives a human being...
When you believe in something, go for it.
Believe in it, and go for it."*

_____

THE POWER OF INTENTION

"Our intention creates our reality."

— WAYNE DYER

Expectation creates the belief, but intention directs that belief into action. If expectation and self-belief are the drivers of success, intention is the force that steers them, ensuring your energy and focus align with your goals.

If "intention" is "to stretch toward", then setting an intention is more than just wishing for success; it's about deliberately stretching your focus, thoughts, and energy in the direction of your goals.

Dr. Wayne Dyer, author of *The Power of Intention*, believed that intention is not just something we do, but a force we align with. He wrote:

"The more you see yourself as what you'd like to become, and act as if what you want is already there, the more you'll activate those dormant forces that will collaborate to transform your dream into your reality."

Neuroscience supports this idea. When you set a clear intention, your Reticular Activating System filters relevant information, helping you notice opportunities that align with your focus. Think of when you decide to buy a specific car; you suddenly start seeing it everywhere. It was always there, but now your mind is focused on it.

How to Strengthen Your Intentions:

- **Define what you want with clarity.**
  The brain thrives on specificity.

- **Act as if success is inevitable.**
  When you expect a result, your actions follow.

- **Reinforce your intention daily.**
  Use visualisation, positive feelings, and journaling.

- **Detach from the outcome.**
  Trust the process without forcing results.

When you combine strong expectations with clear intentions, you train your brain to seek out and act on opportunities that align with your goals. Whether you are an athlete, entrepreneur, or a leader, this principle is a game-changer in creating impact and elevating performance.

I have seen this firsthand with numerous clients. Take Peter, for example. When we worked on the power of intention, I encouraged him to set a clear daily focus, not just on what he wanted, but on how he wanted to show up. In the space of a few days, he found the perfect employee, uncovered two unexpected business opportunities, and regained clarity and confidence.

Indeed, many believe that magic happens when you clearly focus on a specific outcome, truly believe in it, and expect it to happen.

Perhaps what we call magic is simply the mind working in perfect alignment with intention?

THE POWER OF ATTENTION

"You become what you give your attention to."

— EPICTETUS.

Setting clear intentions helps focus your attention, but following through requires sustained focus.

The outer circle of the REWIRE Model highlights attention as a crucial component of high performance. In 2015, Microsoft conducted a study suggesting that the average human attention span had decreased from 12 seconds in 2000 to 8 seconds in 2013, blaming digital distractions. However, more recent research questions this claim, indicating that the widely quoted 8-second attention span may be more myth than fact. However, the truth is, we do succumb to distraction, especially in our highly digital world. More recently, psychologist Gloria Mark, in *Attention Span: Finding Focus for a Fulfilling Life*, reveals striking findings from her decades of research into how technology affects concentration.

She says, on average, people spend just 47 seconds on any screen before shifting their focus, and after an interruption, it takes 25 minutes to fully regain their attention to a task. Even more concerning, we interrupt ourselves more often than we are interrupted by others.

These findings highlight why mastering attention is not just about avoiding distractions, it's about reclaiming control of your mind in an age of endless interruptions. High performers don't allow their focus to be hijacked; they take control of it. The ability to direct and sustain attention determines how effectively you execute your intentions and meet your expectations. Attention is a valuable currency. When you invest it wisely, it compounds into powerful results.

How to Strengthen Your Attention:

- **Use Short Two-Minute Attention Resets.**
  Pause throughout the day to breathe deeply (inhale for 6 counts, exhale for 6). Simply focus on your breath. When your mind drifts, gently guide your attention back to your breath. This calms the nervous system and sharpens focus.

- **Minimise Distractions.**
  Protect your focus by setting boundaries around digital interruptions and schedule deep work sessions.

- **Train Your Attention Like a Muscle.**
  Mindfulness and meditation enhance cognitive control, helping you stay present and engaged.

"Bringing back a wandering attention over and over again is the root of will, character, and judgment."

— WILLIAM JAMES

EXPANDING THINKING

When you set clear intentions, focus your attention, and align your actions with what you want, new opportunities and possibilities open up. However, to fully leverage this and create a greater impact, it is important to be curious and expand your thinking. High performers and entrepreneurs do not just act differently; they push their limits as to what is possible. It's exactly how Cameron McEvoy changed his training regime, and how Uber and Airbnb came into fruition. They challenged conventional limits and stretched their thinking beyond what seemed possible.

Dan Sullivan, creator of 10x Thinking, and one of the world's foremost experts on entrepreneurship in action, teaches that instead of asking, *"How can I improve by 10%?"*, great leaders ask, *"What would it take to improve by 10x?"*

This small yet significant shift in focus forces you to rethink assumptions, break old patterns, and create innovative solutions that wouldn't exist in a traditional, linear mindset.

Similarly, Edward de Bono, author of *Six Thinking Hats* and creator of lateral thinking, taught numerous large companies to expand their thinking, remove biases, and make better, well-rounded decisions. The book provides a framework for structured, expansive thinking by deliberately focusing on one aspect.

For example, wearing a white hat focuses on facts, data, and objective information, while a red hat focuses on emotions and intuition.

THE POWER OF DEEP LISTENING

> *"When people talk, listen completely. Most people never listen."*
>
> — ERNEST HEMINGWAY

Expanding your thinking involves not only generating ideas but also improving your listening and interpreting skills.

Great thinkers and leaders know that the best insights often come not from speaking, but from listening with full presence. Most people listen to reply, not to understand. Neuroscience shows that deep, intentional listening builds trust and strengthens relationships.

Marshall Goldsmith captures this powerfully:

> *"Listening is an art. When people are speaking, they require our undivided attention. We focus on them; we listen very carefully. We listen to the spoken words and the unspoken messages. This means looking directly at the person, eyes connected; we forget we have a watch, just focusing for that moment on that person. It's called respect, it's called appreciation — and it's called leadership."*

Great leaders listen closely, which helps them learn and understand others better, leading to a greater impact.

As Dr. Joe Dispenza notes:

> *"Conscious thoughts, repeated often enough, become unconscious thinking."*

This means that by intentionally changing how you think, asking better and open-ended questions, you can rewire your brain so that one day, it's normal and natural to be an innovative, solution-oriented, and adaptable thinker.

HOW TO TRAIN YOUR MIND FOR 10x THINKING

> *"Logic will get you from A to B. Imagination will take you everywhere."*
>
> — ALBERT EINSTEIN

Challenge assumptions. Instead of accepting limits, ask: *"What if the opposite were true?"*

Use De Bono's *'Six Thinking Hats'* to refine ideas by exploring different perspectives: logic, emotion, creativity, risk, process, and big-picture thinking.

Reframe challenges. Ask yourself, *"How would an innovator or disruptor tackle this problem?"*

Apply 10x Thinking. *"What would need to change to achieve results 10x faster or bigger?"* Keep asking open-ended questions to encourage deeper exploration and thinking.

Be fully present when listening. Set an intention to listen fully, and put away distractions and focus.

Take a moment to pause before responding. Resist the urge to rush in with advice.

PRIORITISATION

"The key is not to prioritize what's on your schedule, but to schedule your priorities."

— STEPHEN COVEY

With a sharper focus and expanded thinking, the next step is ensuring your energy is directed toward the right actions. Attention without intention leads to distraction, and thinking without prioritisation leads to overwhelm. High performers don't just work hard, they work smart, and make deliberate choices to focus on what truly moves the needle.

The Pareto Principle, or 80/20 Rule, states that 80% of results often come from just 20% of efforts. Identifying and focusing on this vital 20% is key to maximising impact. To refine priorities even further, the Eisenhower Matrix provides a structured way to determine which tasks deserve attention.

Named after President Dwight D. Eisenhower, this method was inspired by his legendary ability to make tough decisions efficiently. As a five-star general and later the U.S. president, he had to constantly determine what required his direct attention and what could be delegated. His method became widely embraced as a cornerstone of time management and strategic leadership. Later, popularised by Stephen Covey, it remains a trusted tool for cutting through noise, avoiding unnecessary urgency, and focusing on what truly drives long-term success.

The Eisenhower Matrix categorises tasks into four quadrants:

1. **Urgent and Important.**
   Handle immediately (crises, deadlines).

2. **Important but Not Urgent.**
   Schedule and prioritise (strategy, planning, growth).

3. **Urgent but Not Important.**
   Delegate or automate (emails, interruptions).

4. **Neither Urgent nor Important.**
   Eliminate (distractions, low-value tasks).

Spending more time in Quadrant 2 (Important but Not Urgent) helps you invest in long-term success and allows you to free up mental and emotional energy to focus on what truly matters.

1. **Ask, *"Does this align with my highest priorities?"***
   If not, delegate or eliminate.

2. **Be proactive, not reactive.**
   Focus on strategy, not just immediate demands.

3. **Limit time on low-impact tasks.**
   Many "urgent" tasks are distractions in disguise.

MANAGING EMOTIONS

"Your brain is not designed to make you happy. Your brain is designed to keep you alive. Happiness is your job."

— LISA FELDMAN BARRETT

Now that you have some key strategies to take intentional action, practice deliberately, and keep focused on what truly matters, it is time to address one of the biggest forces that can steal your attention, impact your results, and shape your life — your emotional state.

As you read earlier, the end result of a thought is an emotion, meaning that whatever runs through your mind will determine how you feel. Consider a day when you are dealing with a major work problem. Your mind fixates on the issue, replaying scenarios and conversations. Your energy becomes scattered, and you may feel anxious or on edge. This mental and emotional state impacts your productivity, clarity, and ability to take effective action.

To achieve the best outcomes and perform at your highest level, emotional regulation is non-negotiable. Even with the best of intentions and clear priorities, if your emotions spiral under pressure, your performance will suffer. Fear, stress, anxiety, or even overexcitement, often lumped together under the term stress, can derail even the most disciplined thinker.

UNDERSTANDING STRESS

Stress is often seen as a negative force, but not all stress is bad. In fact, stress is simply your body's response to something that matters to you.

As psychologist Kelly McGonigal defines it:

> *"Stress is what happens to the brain and body when something you care about is at stake."*

Understanding this can help reframe stress as a signal, rather than an enemy. Instead of seeing it as something to avoid, you can view it as a tool for growth and heightened awareness. That said, chronic, unmanaged stress can drain energy, cloud judgment, and weaken decision-making, making it crucial to develop strategies to manage it effectively.

Like any emotion, stress expands when you focus on it. If left unchecked, it can trigger a downward spiral. However, just as a baby can move from crying to laughter when distracted, you, too, can shift your emotional state through conscious interruption, pausing, breathing, or reframing the situation.

Client Story: Shifting Energy

For instance, my client Jakob thrived in high energy of being with people, excelling in sales and leadership. However, he avoided structure and systems, a lower, and slower energy. Slowing down to focus on the details felt uncomfortable, so he frequently avoided such tasks. This avoidance was impacting his long-term success.

To help him embrace the habit of slowing down to focus on a detailed task, I encouraged him to pause for two minutes several times a day, simply focusing on his breath. At first, he resisted, finding it uncomfortable to stop and do nothing. But once he committed to the habit, the results spoke for themselves. He became calmer, more present, and more intentional with his energy. The impact extended beyond him, his team noticed the shift, his leadership influence grew, he easily attracted more clients, and his business flourished.

High performance is not just about how you think, it is also about how you feel and respond under pressure, how you manage your emotional energy under pressure.

Emotions shape neural pathways, reinforcing patterns that either propel you forward or keep you stuck. Mastering your emotions is therefore key to rewiring your brain for lasting change.

BEFRIENDING FEAR

If stress signals that something matters, fear is often the roadblock that keeps you from moving forward. Yet most people instinctively fight or resist fear, which only makes it stronger. Neuroscientist Karin Roelofs, an expert in emotion regulation, found that individuals who learn to manage their emotional responses perform better under pressure. When emotions are regulated effectively, people remain composed, think more clearly, and make stronger decisions.

Fear, like any other emotion, expands when you focus on it. The more you resist, the more power it holds. Instead of trying to eliminate fear, the key is to redirect it, a skill that elite performers use to achieve success.

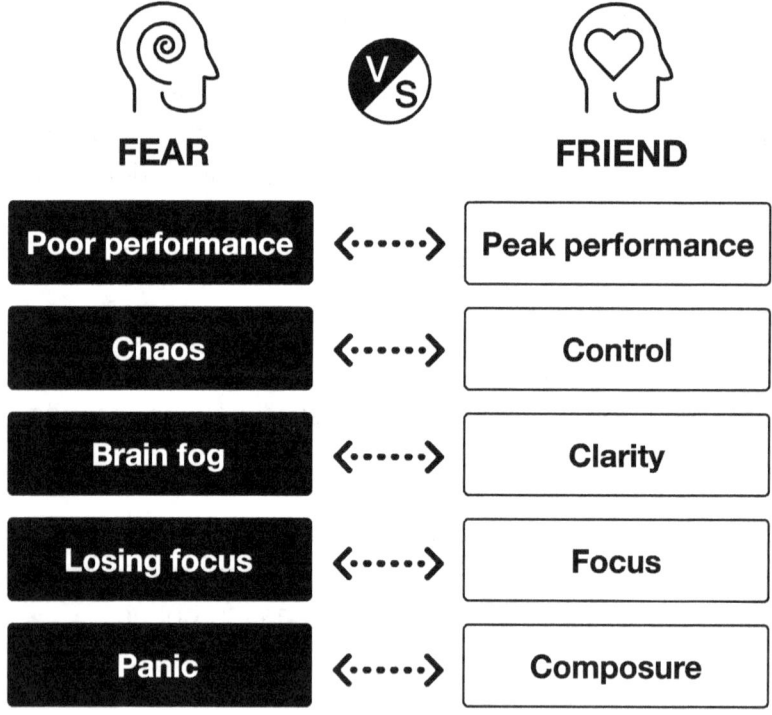

Take Rhiannon Iffland, a world champion cliff diver. Standing atop a 22-metre platform, she faces the moment where fear grips her mind. But rather than resisting it, she befriends her fear. Instead of fixating on the fear, she shifts her focus to trust in her training and abilities. The fear dissipates, replaced by laser-sharp focus and confidence. She takes a deep breath, counts down: three, two, one, and leaps.

This is the same approach I used when battling strong winds in Hawaii. Instead of resisting them, I reframed them. I created my own mantra: *"The wind is my friend."*

Michael Singer, author of *The Untethered Soul*, describes this concept perfectly:

"If you are resisting something,
you are feeding it.
Any energy you fight,
you are feeding.
If you are pushing something away,
you are inviting it to stay."

When you stop resisting and start redirecting fear, you gain composure, clarity, and the ability to perform at your best. This mindset shift allows you to navigate challenges with confidence, adapt quickly, and use fear as a source of energy rather than a barrier to success.

PRACTICAL STRATEGIES TO MANAGE STRESS

To move from reaction to regulation, use these science-backed strategies to reset your emotional state:

- **Name it to tame it.**
  Labelling your emotions reduces their intensity and helps to regain control. Instead of saying, *"I am overwhelmed,"* say, *"I am experiencing stress because this project matters to me."*

- **Anchor yourself with breathwork.**
  Practice the simple breathing technique I mentioned earlier. Inhale for six, exhale for six. If your thoughts distract you, gently guide your attention back to your breath. Saying the word "calm" with each breath positively influences your nervous system, reinforcing a sense of ease.

- **Reframe the situation.**
  Shift your perspective by asking a different question. *"How else can I view this? What positive meanings can I create?"*

- **Choose a go-to strategy.**
  Experiment with different techniques and commit to the one that best works for you, whether it's one of the above, exercise, mindfulness, journaling, or simply stepping away for a mental reset.

MINDFULNESS AND MEDITATION

Managing stress in the moment is essential, but true emotional mastery comes from developing habits that create long-term stability. Just as training the body strengthens physical endurance, training the mind through mindfulness and meditation builds resilience, sharpens focus, and enhances overall well-being

Mindfulness is about being fully present and aware in the moment. It strengthens your attention muscle, increasing emotional regulation and reducing stress.

John Kabat-Zinn defines mindfulness as:

―――――――――――

"The awareness that arises through paying attention, on purpose, in the present moment, non-judgmentally."

―――――――――――

Practicing mindfulness throughout the day helps you become more aware of your emotional state, allowing you to respond rather than react. Attention is a key element of the REWIRE Model's Outer Circle, shaping how we engage with the world, influencing our results and impact.

Meditation, on the other hand, is a structured practice that enhances self-awareness, impulse control, and cognitive flexibility. Studies show that meditation strengthens the prefrontal cortex, improving focus and emotional resilience. Even 2-5 minutes of daily meditation can:

- Improve focus and mental clarity
- Lower cortisol (the stress hormone)
- Increase resilience under pressure

By cultivating mindfulness and meditation, you develop the ability to regulate emotions, stay composed, and enhance leadership and impact.

YAWNING: A SIMPLE YET POWERFUL BRAIN RESET

> *"Yawning is one of the most effective ways to reduce physical, emotional, and neurological stress."*
>
> — MARK WALDMAN

Surprisingly, one of the fastest ways to reduce stress and sharpen focus is something we do naturally: yawning. According to Mark Waldman, a leading researcher in network neuroscience, yawning can instantly restore mental clarity and optimise brain function. More than 60 studies highlight its benefits, including:

- Slowing down excessive activity in the prefrontal cortex.
- Interrupting negative thought patterns and rumination.
- Increasing cerebral blood flow for sharper thinking and decision-making.

Yawning acts as a cooling system for the brain, restoring clarity and balance. Waldman suggests practising three mindful yawns to experience an immediate shift in mood and cognition. For even greater benefits, pair yawning with the deep breathing technique mentioned earlier. This approach has been shown to activate over 1,000 immune-enhancing genes and 1,200 stress-reducing genes.

> For a step-by-step technique that combines yawning with breathwork and mindfulness, visit the **REWIRE Resource Portal**.

HARNESSING STRENGTHS FOR GREATER IMPACT

---

*"Our strengths are not just what we're good at,
they're what energise us.
That's where growth and fulfilment begin."*

— ALEX LINLEY

As well as emotional mastery, another key area that helps us build resilience and our core energy is understanding our strengths. In Chapter Six, I shared an exercise to help you track back along your timeline and identify key strengths. Revisiting them regularly and uncovering unrealised strengths can elevate your success.

Over the years, I've discovered that certain profiling tools have been instrumental in helping my clients and myself gain clarity, improve performance, and maximise impact.

These are three of my favourites, and ones I have personally gained great insights from.

The Enneagram: Understanding Core Motivations

The Enneagram is a personality system that reveals the emotional drivers behind our behaviours, how we engage with others, and what fuels our decision-making. It categorises individuals into nine types, each with a dominant motivation, fear, and way of interacting with the world.

These nine types are grouped into three centres of intelligence:

- Head Types (Driven by logic and fear)
- Heart Types (Driven by emotion and connection)
- Body Types (Driven by instinct and control)

Understanding my Enneagram type helped me gain insight into my natural patterns, how I process challenges, and how I can optimise my strengths while managing my blind spots. For many of my clients, it has been a powerful tool in deepening self-awareness and strengthening emotional intelligence.

Wealth Dynamics: Finding Your Flow and Energy Frequency

Developed by Roger Hamilton, Wealth Dynamics helps individuals and teams discover where they perform at their best, what type of work fuels them, and what tasks drain their energy. Instead of focusing purely on personality, it introduces four energy frequencies that drive performance:

- **Dynamo (Spring, Wood):**
  Innovation, creativity, big-picture thinking

- **Blaze (Summer, Fire):**
  Communication, relationships, influence

- **Tempo (Autumn, Earth):**
  Timing, process, rhythm, connection

- **Steel (Winter, Metal):**
  Precision, detail, systems, analysis

When I first took this profile, I had a lightbulb moment. I realised why I thrive in Dynamo and Blaze energy, coaching, creating, and strategy, but find detailed, repetitive Steel tasks draining. This insight helped me delegate tasks that drained my energy and structure my work to stay in flow, increasing both my productivity and enjoyment. If you want to understand your natural strengths and energy flow, this tool is invaluable.

Kolbe A: How You Take Action

Unlike other assessments that focus on personality or strengths, the Kolbe A Index measures your conative strengths, your natural, instinctive way of taking action. It reveals how you are wired to approach tasks, make decisions, and get things done without overthinking or relying on learned behaviours.

What makes Kolbe A unique is that, as Kathy Kolbe discovered, while personality traits evolve, your conative instincts remain constant throughout life. Her research has been used by Fortune 500 companies, government leaders, and top universities to improve performance and decision-making.

Understanding my Kolbe profile helped me lean into my natural way of working instead of forcing myself into methods that drained my energy. If you have ever felt resistance when tackling certain tasks, this tool can provide valuable insights into how to work smarter, not harder.

LEVERAGING WHAT YOU DO BEST

As outlined in *The Strengths Profile Book* by Alex Linley and Trudy Bateman, research shows that individuals who actively use their strengths experience:

- Greater happiness and confidence.
- Increased resilience and lower stress.
- Higher levels of energy and motivation.
- Improved goal achievement and workplace performance.

A key takeaway from this model is the distinction between:

- **Realised Strengths:**
  What you are good at and love doing.
- **Unrealised Strengths:**
  Hidden potential waiting to be tapped into.
- **Learned Behaviours:**
  Skills that serve you but do not energise you.
- **Weaknesses:**
  Areas that drain you and should be minimised.

One of the most valuable lessons in high performance is that success is not just about doing what you are good at, it is about doing what energises you. High performers spend 70% of their time in their strengths, making intentional choices to minimise work that drains them.

By understanding your natural strengths, energy flow, and conative instincts, you can create an environment where you work at your highest level, avoid burnout, and unlock your full potential

Leadership in Action: A Client's Journey

Derek came to me feeling overwhelmed and constantly reactive, caught in the relentless pressures of managing a massive new sporting stadium project. The demands of multiple stakeholders, ongoing challenges, and decision fatigue were draining his mental, emotional, and physical energy, highlighting how misaligned energy impacts performance, as explored in the Value Model. He was constantly putting out fires, struggling to focus, and losing confidence in his ability to lead effectively.

Through our work together, we focused on clarity, consistency, and intentional leadership. We introduced reflection habits to help him step back from reactive decision-making and ask better questions, an essential shift in rewiring thought patterns and strengthening consistent, empowering behaviours. By prioritising high-impact tasks, managing his energy more effectively, and adopting strategic pauses before reacting, he regained control over his emotions and leadership approach.

Over time, these small but deliberate shifts compounded. Derek transformed from a reactive leader into a proactive, strategic decision-maker. He reclaimed his confidence, improved communication with stakeholders, and created a more empowered, focused team, demonstrating how mastering energy, attention, and prioritisation enhances leadership impact.

Leadership is not about controlling outcomes; it is about influencing through presence, energy, and example. By mastering fear, managing stress, optimising energy, expanding thinking, and deeply listening, you elevate your leadership to a level where your impact extends far beyond yourself.

THE POWER OF SELF-CARE

An obvious, yet often neglected area of our lives is taking care of ourselves. Yet frequently, people are too 'busy' to take this important topic seriously. They tend to keep pushing until something happens to make them slow down.

Your brain and body are your greatest assets, and taking care of them is non-negotiable for sustained success.

Dr. Daniel Amen, a leading brain health expert, emphasises:

*"Your brain's health determines
how you think, feel, and act.
Protect it, and you protect your future."*

Optimal performance requires more than just mental resilience, it is built on a strong foundation of physical, emotional, and cognitive well-being.

The Essentials: Sleep, Exercise and Fuel

*Want to perform at your best?
Start with sunlight, sleep, and movement."*

— DR. ANDREW HUBERMAN

Sleep:
Quality sleep is critical for memory, decision-making, and emotional regulation. Research shows that chronic sleep deprivation impairs cognitive function as much as alcohol intoxication. Prioritise at least 7-9 hours of deep, restorative sleep to enhance focus and performance.

Exercise:
Regular movement boosts brain function, enhances mood by increasing endorphins, dopamine, and serotonin, and improves stress tolerance. Even a 20-minute walk can sharpen mental clarity, stimulate creativity, and support brain health.

Nutrition
The foods you eat directly impact cognitive performance. A brain-healthy diet rich in omega-3s, antioxidants, and whole foods supports focus, mood, and long-term brain health.

THE HEALING POWER OF NATURE

*"Look deep into nature,
and then you will understand everything better."*

— ALBERT EINSTEIN

Spending time in nature is one of the most powerful ways to reset your mind and body. Research shows that even 20 minutes outside three times a week can reduce stress, improve cognitive function, and lower cortisol levels.

Longer exposure deepens the benefits. A study in Finland found that city dwellers who spent at least five hours in nature per month reported higher well-being, reduced anxiety, and improved overall life satisfaction.

For deeper benefits, longer nature experiences help restore energy and boost resilience. Studies have found that military veterans who participated in four-day white-water rafting trips experienced a 29% reduction in PTSD symptoms and a 21% decrease in stress levels.

For those who cannot take extended time off, the Japanese practice of Shinrin-yoku, or forest bathing, offers a simple yet powerful solution. Walking mindfully in nature lowers blood pressure, reduces anxiety, and strengthens the immune system, proving that even short, intentional time in nature can be transformative.

Beyond well-being, experiencing awe in nature shifts our perspective. In a study at the University of California, Irvine, researcher Paul Piff found that participants who spent just 60 seconds looking up at towering trees reported increased feelings of awe and were more likely to help a stranger than those who viewed an equally tall but uninspiring building.

"Experiences of awe attune people to things larger than themselves," explains Piff. *"They cause individuals to feel less entitled, less selfish, and to behave in more generous and helping ways."*

THE POWER OF PLAY

"The opposite of play is not work. It's depression."

— DR. STUART BROWN

Play is not just for children, it is a biological necessity for creativity, problem-solving, and emotional resilience. Neuroscience confirms that play strengthens neuroplasticity, forming new neural connections that enhance learning and adaptability.

Dr. Stuart Brown, founder of the National Institute for Play, found that play-deprived adults experience more stress, burnout, and rigid thinking, while those who engage in regular play are more adaptable, innovative, and emotionally resilient.

Some of the world's top performers, from Albert Einstein to Warren Buffett, incorporated play into their routines to enhance creativity and sustain high performance.

- **Enhances Creativity:**
  Play activates the brain's imagination and problem-solving networks.

- **Reduces Stress:**
  Engaging in fun activities lowers cortisol and boosts dopamine.

- **Improves Emotional Resilience:**
  Play helps process emotions and recover from setbacks.

- **Boosts Brain Rewiring:**
  Play strengthens the brain's adaptability and cognitive flexibility.

Now you understand the power of nature and benefits of play, how can you add more of these into your life?

Prioritising Self-Care for Maximum Impact

"Almost everything will work again if you unplug it for a few minutes — including you."

— ANNE LAMOTT

High performance is not just about pushing harder, it is about replenishing energy strategically. Whether through sleep, movement, mindful time in nature, or play, self-care fuels clarity, consistency, and impact. By making these habits a priority, you build a strong foundation for long-term success and resilience.

SELF-CARE IN ACTION: ROWENA'S STORY

One of my long-term clients, Rowena, thrived in a high-pressure leadership role in the mining industry, yet she constantly felt overwhelmed and drained. As a Mechanic profile in Wealth Dynamics, she had a natural brilliance for optimising systems and solving problems. However, this strength led her to take on too much responsibility, overworking herself while neglecting her own needs.

She was stuck in the belief that she had to prove herself to feel "good enough." Her stress levels were high, and self-care was always her last priority.

Through our work together, we focused on:

- Energy management strategies to help her sustain peak performance.
- Pausing and breathing techniques to break the cycle of stress.
- Creating POSTs (Positive Statements) to reframe limiting beliefs.
- Asking better questions to redefine responsibility and balance.

As a result, she became calmer, more focused, and began prioritising herself. She also initiated an honest conversation with her boss about her workload, which led to a promotion and greater recognition for her leadership.

Rowena's transformation highlights a powerful truth: when you prioritise your well-being, your impact expands.

To help you maintain balance and boost your energy, I've created the Circle of Wellbeing, a simple yet powerful model to guide you in identifying what you most need right now, whether mental, emotional, physical or social.

> You can download your own copy from the **REWIRE Resources Portal**.

Leading with Impact: What People Need Most

In his research, Peter Kaufman identified five core desires that drive human behaviour:

- **To be appreciated** — Genuine recognition fosters loyalty and engagement.
- **To be respected** — Feeling valued leads to greater commitment.
- **To feel heard** — Active listening builds trust and motivation.
- **To have autonomy** — Empowering individuals increases ownership.
- **To experience growth** — People thrive in environments that challenge and develop them.

Great leaders understand that creating impact is not just about what you do, it is about how you make people feel. When individuals feel valued, supported, and empowered, they perform at their best.

But sustaining this level of impact requires more than skill and strategy, it demands effective energy management.

ENERGY MANAGEMENT

Tony Schwartz, author of *The Power of Full Engagement*, emphasises that energy, not time, is the fundamental currency of high performance. Leaders who optimise their energy, not just their schedules, create sustainable success.

Schwartz categorises energy into four dimensions:

- **Physical Energy:**
  Nutrition, movement, and sleep fuel peak performance.

- **Emotional Energy:**
  Positive emotions drive engagement and resilience.

- **Mental Energy:**
  Focus and attention sharpen decision-making.

- **Spiritual Energy:**
  Purpose-driven work fuels long-term motivation.

By identifying and eliminating energy drainers, such as unnecessary meetings, toxic relationships, or mental clutter, leaders free up energy for high-value actions that create greater impact.

True leadership is not about perfection; it is about showing up, staying aligned with your values, and continuously evolving. When you manage your energy, strengthen emotional intelligence, and listen with intention, you build influence, create stronger teams, and leave a lasting legacy.

SELF-ACTUALISATION

"In any given moment we have two options: to step forward into growth or to step back into safety."

— ABRAHAM MASLOW

Throughout this book, you have strengthened your mindset, refined your focus, and aligned your actions to create clarity, consistency, and impact. You have developed the ability to adapt, manage your energy, expand your thinking, and lead with intention. Each step has moved you toward a higher level of personal mastery.

Psychologist Abraham Maslow described self-actualisation as the highest level of human development — the point at which we fully express our potential, creativity, and purpose. It is not just about personal success; it is about becoming the best version of yourself and using your growth to positively influence others.

Maslow's Hierarchy of Needs outlines five stages of human development, progressing from basic survival to self-actualisation.

By integrating these principles, you are on the path to self-actualisation — where you not only realise your full potential but also inspire and impact those around you.

The journey through this book aligns with these stages, guiding you toward fulfilling your highest potential:

1. **Physiological Needs**
(Survival and Energy Management)
   a. Managing physical energy, health, and well being
   b. Understanding how mindset affects performance

2. **Safety Needs**
(Stability and Resilience)
   a. Overcoming fear and self-doubt
   b. Strengthening mental resilience and adaptability

3. **Love and Belonging**
(Connection and Influence)
   a. Building stronger relationships through communication and leadership
   b. Using energy and presence to create impact

4. **Esteem Needs**
(Confidence and Mastery)
   a. Developing clarity and consistency in actions
   b. Practicing purposeful habits to build self-belief

5. **Self-Actualisation**
(Becoming Your Best Self)
   a. Fully embodying the REWIRE Model principles
   b. Using your growth to elevate others and create meaningful impact

This is not just about what you achieve but who you become in the process. When you reach this stage, your impact extends beyond yourself, influencing those around you and creating lasting change.

Maslow emphasised that self-actualisation is not a fixed destination; it is a continuous process of growth, mastery, and contribution. The more you cultivate clarity, consistency, and impact, the more you expand into the highest expression of yourself.

FINAL THOUGHTS

When you show up fully, honour your potential, and commit to growth, you do not just transform your own life — you create a ripple effect that inspires and elevates those around you. That is the true power of impact.

"When you let your own light shine, you unconsciously give others permission to do the same."

— MARIANNE WILLIAMSON

KEY INSIGHTS

✓ **Your Expectations Shape Your Reality.**
High expectations drive high performance. When you believe in your ability to succeed, you take bold actions and push past limits. Eliud Kipchoge's philosophy, "No Human Is Limited," demonstrates the power of self-belief.

✓ **Energy Management is the Foundation of Sustainable Success.**
Your ability to manage physical, emotional, and mental energy determines your capacity to lead, think clearly, and sustain results. Simple practices like breathwork, mindfulness, and intentional recovery help regulate stress and sharpen focus.

✓ **Self-Actualisation is a Continuous Process.**
True impact comes from continuously expanding your potential. By managing your energy, emotions, and mindset, you elevate yourself, and those around you

✓ **Alignment Unlocks Self-Actualisation.**
According to Maslow, your highest growth comes when your thoughts, emotions, and actions are in harmony. When you align with your purpose, you move beyond achievement into meaningful contribution and lasting influence.

ACTION STEPS

- **Ask Better Questions.**
  Before reacting, pause and ask yourself: What is the best way to respond? What really matters here? The quality of your questions determines the quality of your decisions.

- **Breathe to Master Your Emotional State.**
  Pause for one to two minutes every hour and take conscious, deep breaths.
  This resets your nervous system, sharpens focus, and helps you respond rather than react.

- **Prioritise Play and Nature.**
  Choose one playful activity this week — movement, creativity, or laughter.
  Also, commit to one outdoor activity to refresh your mind.

- **Practice Deep Listening.**
  In your next conversation, set the intention to truly listen without interrupting.
  Pay full attention and notice how it strengthens connection and understanding.

- **Use Your Tools Consistently.**
  Tools like the Circle of Wellbeing aren't just for when things go wrong.
  They're here to help you stay aligned with what you need — mentally, emotionally, and physically, every day.

CHAPTER 9:
The Path Forward

"The privilege of a lifetime is to become who you truly are."

— CARL JUNG

THE STORY OF THE EARTH SCHOOL

Creator gathered all of creation and said, *"I want to hide something from the humans until they are ready for it. It is the knowledge that they create their own reality."*

"Give it to me," said the salmon. *"I will hide it on the bottom of the ocean."*

"No," said the Creator. *"One day, they will go to the bottom of the ocean and find it."*

"Give it to me," said the eagle. *"I will take it to the moon."*

"No," said the Creator. *"One day, they will go to the moon and find it."*

"Then I will bury it deep in the earth," said the mole.

"No," said the Creator. *"One day, they will dig deep into the earth and find it."*

Then Grandmother Mole, who lives deep in the earth and sees with her heart, said, *"Put it inside them. They will never think to look there."*

And so it was done.

And there lies the secret. Our senses are designed to look outwards.

You Hold the Key to Your Growth

This story is a powerful reminder that the answers we seek have always been within us. Yet, the challenge is that we do not always see them clearly. We don't see the world as it is, we see it through the lens of our past experiences, beliefs, and neural patterns. Our brains filter reality, often reinforcing old ways of thinking that can keep us stuck. This is why transformation is not something external, it is an inside-out process. If you only take into account what happens outside of you, you are not seeing the whole picture.

Throughout this book, you have explored the REWIRE Model, strengthening your mindset, refining your focus, and aligning your actions with clarity, consistency, and impact. You have begun the process of rewiring your brain, expanding your mindset, and stepping into a higher version of yourself.

But transformation is not a single event, it is an ongoing journey.

As Maslow emphasised, self-actualisation is not a fixed destination; it is a continuous process of growth, mastery, and contribution. The more you cultivate clarity, consistency, and impact, the more you expand into the highest expression of yourself. However, sustaining this transformation requires guidance, structure, and support.

Like Kellie, your growth is not about perfection, it's about alignment. With the right structure, support, and intention, you can evolve into your next level of leadership and fulfilment. That's exactly what the CLEAR Coaching Model is designed to support.

THE CLEAR COACHING MODEL: A FRAMEWORK FOR CONTINUED GROWTH

Through my experience coaching high performers and navigating my own transformation, I developed the CLEAR Model, a structured yet flexible framework for lasting change. It is my proprietary system designed to help you navigate growth, overcome obstacles, and create a high-performance mindset. This model gives you a practical framework to help you take action and sustain your transformation, ensuring that you stay aligned with your highest vision. Whether you are a leader, an entrepreneur, or simply someone committed to personal excellence, the CLEAR model will help you navigate the continuous process of growth, move through challenges, and take empowered action.

The model is represented as a circle, symbolising the continuous nature of growth. At its core is identity, your core energy, because who you are at the deepest level influences everything you do. The arrows moving in different directions represent the process of letting go of outdated patterns while simultaneously creating new, empowering ones. Each element of the model interacts with and reinforces the others, supporting lasting transformation.

Just as the US Navy spends millions annually removing barnacles from ships to prevent them from slowing down or veering off course, we must remove the mental and emotional burdens that hold us back. The CLEAR Model ensures that you continue to move forward with purpose and alignment, rather than staying stuck in old habits and patterns.

It builds upon the foundation of the REWIRE Model, providing a structured yet flexible framework for continuous growth. While the REWIRE Model helps you shift your mindset, reprogram limiting beliefs, and create new patterns for success, the CLEAR Model takes it further by helping you reinforce, integrate and sustain these changes over time.

Growth is not linear, it's cyclical. That's why you can enter the CLEAR Model at any stage, whether you need clarity, want to remove internal obstacles, take aligned action, or to refine your approach. Every part of the model feeds the next, just as in the REWIRE Model, where clarity, consistency, and impact are interconnected.

Coaching within this framework allows for targeted focus on what will create the greatest shift while ensuring that your transformation lasts.

This is why many of my clients work with me for years, not because they are broken, but because as they grow, new levels of possibility open up, bringing new challenges that require further evolution.

One of my long-term clients, Kellie, initially came to me seeking skills to grow her confidence and manage the pressures of her job. As she gained clarity around her values and strengths, and learned to regulate her emotions, her self-belief grew. With time, she found the courage to pursue a long-held dream and start her own practice.

As her responsibilities expanded, new challenges emerged, such as managing a team and complex client proposals and investments.

By working through each phase of the CLEAR Model, Kellie continually aligned with her vision and purpose. With every step, she strengthened her self-belief, deepened her clarity, and elevated her impact.

THE FIVE ELEMENTS OF THE CLEAR MODEL OF COACHING

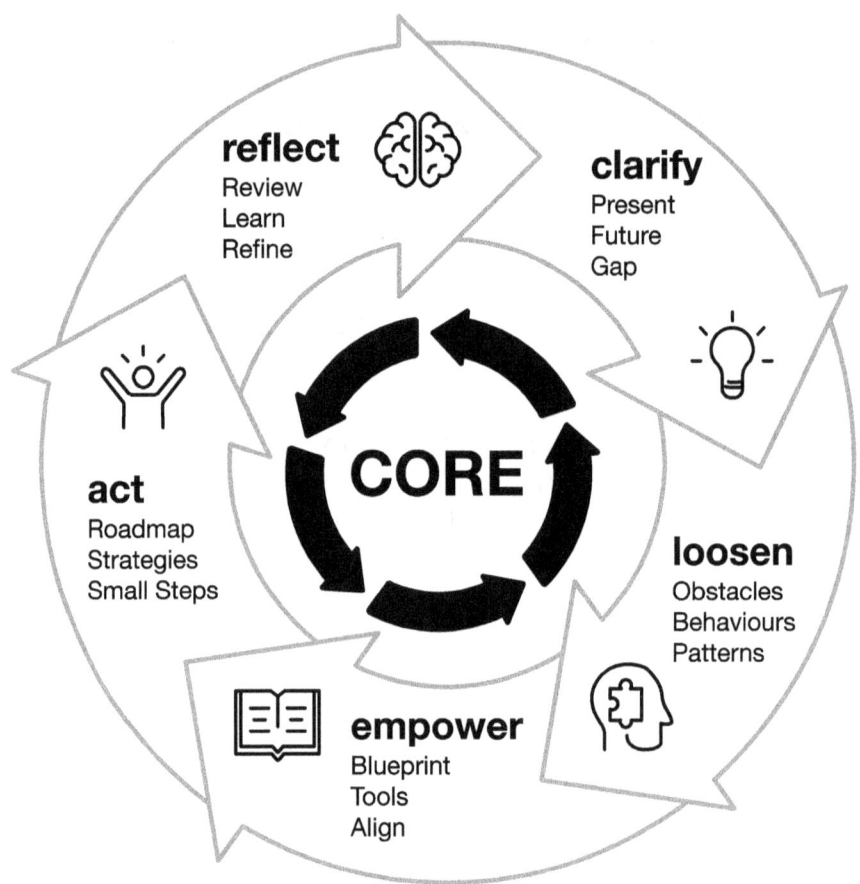

CLARIFY

The first step is to understand your current situation by identifying where you are now (PRESENT), where you want to be (FUTURE), and what is holding you back (GAP). Clarity is the foundation for growth and the compass that guides all meaningful action.

LOOSEN

Release obstacles, unwanted behaviours, and limiting patterns that have been hindering your progress. This is where you start to rewire your mindset, shedding the beliefs and habits that no longer serve you.

EMPOWER

Create a new blueprint with the right tools and align your conscious and subconscious mind to ensure lasting change. True empowerment comes when your thoughts, emotions, and actions are working in harmony.

ACT

Action leads to results. Here, we create a clear roadmap with effective strategies and take small steps consistently to achieve incremental progress and desired outcomes. Without action, even the best insights remain just ideas.

REFLECT

Reflection is crucial for growth. Regularly review what is working and what is not, learn from your experiences, and refine your approach to stay aligned with your goals. The most successful individuals are those who continuously assess and improve.

At the heart of the model is your CORE Energy — your identity shaped by your values, beliefs, attitudes, feelings, and behaviours. Through coaching, you evolve into a more empowered version of yourself, gaining control, awareness, and alignment on the path to self-actualisation.

Just like compound interest, small, consistent changes lead to significant, lasting results over time.

NEXT STEPS

Personal transformation is not a one-time decision; it is a commitment to continuous growth. The question is: what will you do next?

If you are ready to step up and know you can do this better with support, I invite you to reach out. Coaching is not just about solving problems; it is about creating opportunities, accelerating progress, and ensuring you are living in alignment with your highest vision.

Today, more than ever, we need people to step into their potential, influence others positively, and be the change they wish to see in the world. And to do this, cultivating a high-performance mindset is essential.

"Every problem, every dilemma, every dead end we find ourselves facing in life, only appears unsolvable inside a particular frame or point of view. Enlarge the box, or create another frame around the data, and problems vanish, while new opportunities appear."

— BENJAMIN ZANDER, *THE ART OF POSSIBILITY*

If you remember at the beginning, we mentioned that it only takes 0.1% of the population to create a shift. With the power of belief, expectation, and your renewed energy radiating from your core, you have the potential to make a bigger impact than you ever imagined.

As Hillel the Elder wisely asked:

---

*"If not now,
when?"*

The journey does not end here. It is only the beginning. If you are ready to take the next step, I invite you to reach out. Whether you are seeking clarity, wanting to remove limitations, or striving for greater impact, together, we can create the path forward.

---

*"Now is the time to get serious
about living your idea.
How long can you afford to put off
who you really want to be?
Your nobler self cannot wait any longer...
Decide to be extraordinary
and do what you need to do — now."*

— EPICTETUS, *THE ART OF LIVING*

FINAL WORDS

> Remember to visit the **REWIRE Resources Portal**.

- ✓ **Tools** only create change when they're used intentionally and consistently.

- ✓ **You are stronger than you think you are.**

- ✓ **Time is your most precious commodity,** and energy is your most valuable asset. Use both wisely.

- ✓ **Embrace urgency.**
  Your time is limited, so live with purpose, and always strive to be your best.

- ✓ **Get clear on what you want,** and get to know yourself from the inside out.

- ✓ **Create a vision,** set meaningful goals, and take consistent action toward your goals and in alignment with the person you want to become.

- ✓ **Learn to prioritise and master your attention.**
  Don't let it be hijacked.

- ✓ **Be a curious observer of your self-talk, emotions, and behaviours.**
  Awareness is always the first step to change.

- ✓ **Adopt** a mindset of continuous growth and improvement.

- ✓ **Lead by example.**
  When you show up as your best self, you don't just elevate your own life, you inspire others to do the same.

- ✓ **And, of course, be curious and be kind.**

- ✓ **Keep learning, keep growing.**
  And remember, your mind is your most powerful tool — use it well.

This is how you create a high-performance mindset. This is how you change your life, inspire others, and make a bigger impact.

If you reflect back on the VALUE model from Chapter 2, you'll remember that impact sits at the top. It represents the culmination of everything you've learned — when your thoughts, emotions, and actions are aligned, your full potential comes to life. Just as Eliud Kipchoge, Rhiannon Iffland, Claire, Sulaiman, and the other inspiring clients featured in this book have shown, high performance is not reserved for the few, it's available to anyone willing to commit, grow, and lead from within. That means you.

And if you remember, at the very beginning of this journey, I shared a quote from the late Wayne Dyer. It feels fitting to end with it, too:

> *"When you change the way you look at things, the things you look at change."*
>
> — WAYNE DYER

If I can help you in any way, I invite you to reach out and contact me at:

https://mindsetforsuccess.com.au/contact/

About the Author

 Mandy Napier is a High Performance Mindset Coach, educator, and author who has spent nearly two decades helping entrepreneurs, leaders, and high performers rewire their thinking and break through to their next level of impact.

Known as the Mindset Alchemist, she's recognised for her practical, no-fluff approach and laser focus on results.

Her personal story adds depth to her work. She has:

- Represented Australia in ultra-distance triathlons
- Competed in the Hawaiian Ironman World Championships
- Spent six years travelling the globe — often solo — seeking growth, grit, and perspective
- Built a thriving mindset coaching practice that has transformed hundreds of lives

With a background in managing and leading high-performing sales teams for over 20 years, Mandy brings a results-driven yet deeply human approach to helping her clients achieve extraordinary success in life, work, and leadership.

Further Reading

Anders Ericsson,
Peak

Don Miguel Ruiz,
The Four Agreements

Wayne Dyer,
The Power of Intention

Gloria Mark,
Attention Span: Finding Focus for a Fulfilling Life

Edward de Bono,
Six Thinking Hats

Michael Singer,
The Untethered Soul

Alex Linley, Trudy Bateman,
The Strengths Profile Book

Tony Schwartz,
The Power of Full Engagement

Viktor Frankl,
Man's Search for Meaning

Noreena Hertz,
The Lonely Century

Stephen Covey,
The 7 Habits of Highly Effective People

Charles Duhigg,
The Power of Habits

Norman Doidge,
The Brain That Changes Itself

Celeste Kidd, Benjamin Y. Hayden,
The Psychology and Neuroscience of Curiosity

Neville,
The Power of Awareness

Caroline Myss,
Defy Gravity

Dr. Joe Dispensa,
Breaking the Habit of Being You, Beyond Supernatural

Maxwell Maltz,
The New Psycho-Cybernetics

Shankar Vedantam,
The Hidden Brain

Daniel Kahneman,
Thinking, Fast and Slow

Roy F. Baumeister and John Tierney,
Willpower

Paul Bloom,
The Human Mind

Angela Duckworth,
Grit

Jeff Olsen,
The Slight Edge

Serge Kahili King,
Mastering Your Hidden Self

Grant Soosalu and Marvin Oka,
mBraining

Daniel Goleman,
Emotional Intelligence

Lisa Feldman Barrett,
How Emotions Are Made

Want More?

WHETHER YOU'RE A

✓ **high-performing leader**

✓ **entrepreneur**

✓ **athlete**

✓ **or someone committed to personal excellence**

YOUR NEXT LEVEL OF IMPACT STARTS
WITH YOUR MINDSET.

Mandy Napier is a High Performance Mindset Coach, speaker, and author who helps high achievers unlock clarity, consistency, and lasting impact. She's worked with professionals across industries including mining, finance, construction, education, and health — with clients from Flight Centre, BHP, Boart Longyear, Queensland Health, Bank of America, and more.

She is:

- Mindset Coach for Fire Recruitment Australia
- The founding Mindset Coach for a US-based global start-up
- Author of *Creating Healthy Life Habits* and *REWIRE*
- A trusted speaker and trainer for leaders and teams

Popular Speaking Topics:

- **The Winning Edge:** Daily Mindset Habits of High Performers

- **Inside the Mind of a Champion:** Mental Strategies for Peak Performance

- **High Performance Mindset in Uncertain Times:** Tools to Thrive, Not Just Survive

- **Healthy Mind, Healthy Life:** REWIRE for Wellbeing and Success

> Each talk combines neuroscience, coaching strategies, and lived experience to energise, inspire, and equip audiences for sustained performance and greater impact.

Whether you're interested in coaching, speaking, or accessing tools to help you create lasting success, here's how to stay connected:

CONNECT WITH MANDY

CONTACT:

 WEBSITE:
www.mindsetforsuccess.com.au

 EMAIL:
mandy@mindsetforsuccess.com.au

ONLINE ACADEMY:
*Explore courses, tools,
and resources to support your growth:*
academy.mindsetforsuccess.com.au
Short URL: bit.ly/3Rmslke

SOCIAL MEDIA:

 LinkedIn:
linkedin.com/in/mandynapier

 Facebook:
facebook.com/mandynapier61

 Instagram
instagram.com/mandynapier

 YouTube:
youtube.com/@MandyNapier

WORK WITH MANDY

COACHING:
mindsetforsuccess.com.au/mindset-coaching

BOOK MANDY TO SPEAK:
mindsetforsuccess.com.au/speaking

ACCESS THE REWIRE RESOURCES PORTAL
Exclusive downloads, mindset tools, and resources referenced throughout the book.
Scan the QR code
or visit: https://bit.ly/3Rmslke
Tip: Bookmark the page for quick access anytime you need a mindset reset or clarity boost!

OTHER FREE RESOURCES

WEEKLY MINDSET QUESTIONS + TIPS:
mindsetforsuccess.com.au/newsletter

MINDSET ESSENTIALS TOOLKIT (FREE SUCCESS TOOLS)
https://bit.ly/4lyl7Y8

www.ingramcontent.com/pod-product-compliance
Lightning Source LLC
Chambersburg PA
CBHW050339010526
44119CB00049B/613